VIDEO

The Salsa-riffic World of

Spanish

Part 1

VIDEO TIME CODES

0:03:28 **Oh, Yeah. You Can Speak Spanish.**

0:04:56 A: Pronunciation

0:06:22 1. vocabulary

0:11:17 2. the Spanish alphabet

0:13:35 3. the pronunciation of vowels

0:15:25 4. cognates

0:16:30 5. pronunciation of tricky consonants

0:23:57 6. diphthongs

0:28:20 B: Capitalization & Accents

0:28:55 1. vocabulary

0:30:00 2. capitalization

0:30:40 3. the pronoun

0:31:05 4. proper nouns

0:33:48 5. names

0:34:33 6. people's titles

0:34:55 7. book titles

0:36:23 8. written accents

0:39:36 C: The Numbers 0 to 99

0:39:48 1. vocabulary

0:40:33 2. the numbers 0 to 19

0:44:25 3. the multiples of ten

0:45:30 D: Honey, We Need to Talk

0:46:32 1. vocabulary

0:47:47 2. greetings and goodbyes

0:50:30 3. punctuation

0:50:42 a. question marks

0:51:01 b. exclamation marks

Articles and Pronouns 0:51:37

A: Articles 0:51:41

1. vocabulary 0:51:50

2. nouns, articles, and gender 0:52:12

3. definite articles 0:54:00

4. indefinite articles 0:55:51

B: Pronouns 0:57:54

1. second-person pronouns 0:58:45

2. first-person pronouns 1:03:29

3. third-person pronouns 1:04:36

The Verbs *Ser* and *Estar* 1:06:55

A: Using the Verb Ser 1:07:18

1. vocabulary 1:07:25

2. differences between ser and estar 1:09:00

3. conjugating **ser** 1:09:20

4. practice sentences 1:14:01

THE SALSA-RIFFIC WORLD OF SPANISH PARTS 1 & 2 STUDY SIDEKICK

(1ST EDITION)

WRITTEN BY THE STANDARD DEVIANTS® ACADEMIC TEAM, INCLUDING:

Kristie Wingenbach

Esperanza Román-Mendoza

Delores Gómez-Morán

Florencia Gonzales

Rachel Galvin

EDITED BY:

Rachel Galvin

CONTRIBUTING EDITOR:

Jennie Halfant

ART DIRECTION AND GRAPHIC DESIGN BY:

Sarah W. Fry

Heather D. Westhoven

C. Christopher Stevens

ı W. Fry

: Middleton

Reader-friendly. We've bolded all Spanish words and italicized their English translations so it'll be clear which is which.

Learn New Stuff. Unfortunately, we just can't include everything about Spanish in two videos. The **OTHER IMPORTANT STUFF** section gives other cool facts you'll need to ace your tests.

Test Yourself. **QUIZZES** and **PRACTICE EXAMS** allow you to test yourself and make sure you've covered all the bases. The answers appear at the back––*don't cheat!*

Have Fun. The book is chock-full of diversions and stress relievers, a few recipes to tantalize your tastebuds, and there are two neat flippy pictures at the bottom of each page!

TABLE OF CONTENTS

VIDEO NOTES

VIDEO NOTES

OTHER IMPORTANT STUFF

TEST YOURSELF

OH, YEAH. YOU CAN SPEAK SPANISH.

Spanish is spoken by just about a bazillion people around the world. Spanish, like Italian and French, is a Romance language.

Romance languages are derived from Latin, the ancient language of Rome.

Spanish, French, Italian, Portuguese, and Rumanian have many similar words since they are all Romance languages with Latin roots.

The Spaniards brought their language to the Western Hemisphere in 1492, when they first arrived on the island of Hispaniola, which is now Haiti and the Dominican Republic. Today, the Spanish language is spoken in Spain and in 18 countries throughout Latin America.

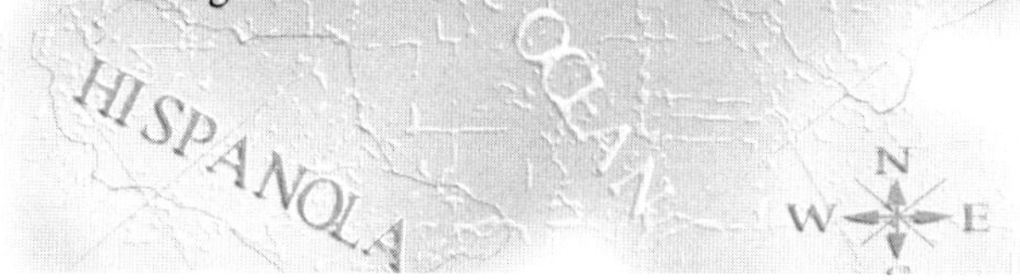

Spanish-Speaking Countries in Latin America

Argentina

Bolivia

Chile

Colombia

Costa Rica

Cuba

The Dominican Republic

Ecuador

El Salvador

Guatemala

Honduras

Mexico

Nicaragua

Panama

Paraguay

Peru

Puerto Rico

Uruguay

Venezuela

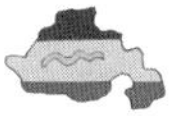

Oh...and Farfalonia. Yeah, right.*

Once you learn Spanish, you can travel, haggle, or write love letters to people in any of these countries!

How Vocabulary Sections Work in This Book

At the beginning of each section, you will find a list of vocabulary words. These vocabulary words may not be the main focus of the section, but you need to know them because:

1. If you're going to speak Spanish, you have to know Spanish words.

2. These are the words we'll use for our examples, and our examples are both crunchy *and* nutritious!

So learn 'em! Check out the Other Important Stuff section for bonus cool and useful Spanish vocabulary words.

Note: When a vocabulary word has two possible endings, one masculine and one feminine, we've put them both in the vocabulary list.

Do not fret, we will explain about that masculine-and-feminine-endings thing later on!

* You probably shouldn't write this on your Spanish exam.

SECTION A: PRONUNCIATION

Vocabulary

la cena - *dinner*
el eructo - *burp*
el pelo - *hair*
muy - *very*
bonito(a) - *pretty*
muy bonito(a) - *very pretty*
el cine - *movie theater*
el idiota - *idiot*
el ojo - *eye*
el ojo morado - *black eye*
la trucha - *trout*
estúpido(a) - *stupid*
la trucha estúpida - *stupid trout*
las consonantes - *consonants*
bueno(a) - *good*
la vaca - *cow*
el burro - *donkey*
la ciudad - *city*
el curso - *course*
la calle - *street*
el coche / el carro - *car*
gracias - *thank you*
el gato - *cat*
el regalo - *gift*

A Tip from Señorita Cortesía:

1. Never burp loudly in public in a Spanish-speaking country. It's considered extremely impolite and people will think you're disgusting.
2. To native Spanish speakers, *idiota* and *estúpido* are pretty serious insults--so use these words judiciously unless you're prepared for a swift kick in the shin.

The Salsa-riffic World of Spanish Part 1

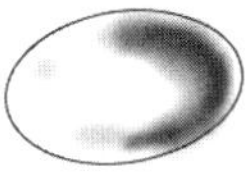

el general - *general*
la magia - *magic*
inteligente - *intelligent*
el guante - *glove*
el garaje - *garage*
gordo - *fat*
la guerra - *war*
la guitarra - *guitar*
el pingüino - *penguin*
la cigüeña - *stork*
la hormiga - *ant*
el huevo - *egg*
ahora - *now*
juntos - *together*
la naranja - *orange (the fruit)*
naranja - *orange (the color)*
joven - *young*
el bolso - *purse*
la llave - *key*

amarillo - *yellow*
el año - *year*
el niño - *little boy*
la uña - *fingernail*
quinto - *fifth*
el queso - *cheese*
querido - *beloved*
el ferrocarril - *railway/train*
rápido - *fast*
la rata - *rat*
rellena - *stuffed*
el zapato - ***shoe***
azúcar - *sugar*
la tetera - *teapot*
no más - *no more*
los cocos- *coconuts*
la justicia humana - *human justice*
el aguacate - *avocado*
siete - *seven*

Now Hear This!

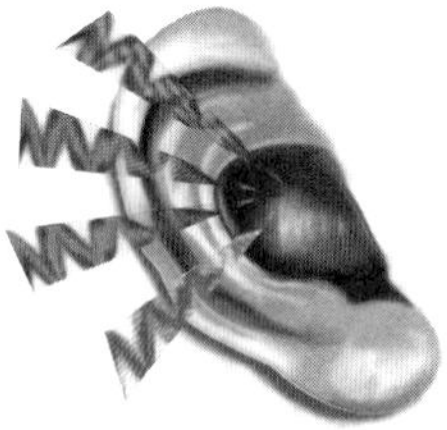

You will be tested on your pronunciation of Spanish--count on it. But don't worry, Spanish is an easy language to pronounce. Start by learning the Spanish alphabet. That shouldn't tax your head too much. It's a little different from the English alphabet, but it won't take you long to get used to it.

We highly recommend that you use this book in conjunction with *The Salsa-riffic World of Spanish Parts 1 and 2* Video Course Reviews. The videos will allow you to get used to how the language sounds and help your pronunciation. Unfortunately, this Study Sidekick can't roll an **r** at you or make that lovely **ñ** sound. However, it is more than willing to listen to you for hours. Here's how to impress the book, win friends, and influence Spanish professors:

4 SURE-FIRE STEPS to turning your tongue SPANISH!

1.

Pop *The Salsa-riffic World of Spanish Parts 1 and 2* into your VCR. (One at a time, please.)

2.

Listen closely to how The Standard Deviants™ pronounce Spanish letters and words.

3.

Repeat all the Spanish you hear in the tapes. Hit PAUSE if you need to untangle your tongue.

4.

When you're using this workbook, practice reading aloud--new words, old words, insults, and compliments alike. The more you practice, the more naturally the Spanish will flow from your tongue. We guarantee that this Study Sidekick will sit patiently and listen to you practice without interrupting or making any judgments.

Do these 4 things and you'll sound like RICARDO MONTALBAN in no time!

THE ALPHABET

The modern Spanish alphabet consists of 27 letters. Yes, 27. We've listed each letter, its name, and an approximation of how to pronounce it. Like we said, the book can't talk back to you and it's hard to accurately *show* you the way something *sounds*, but this quick guide can help you get started.

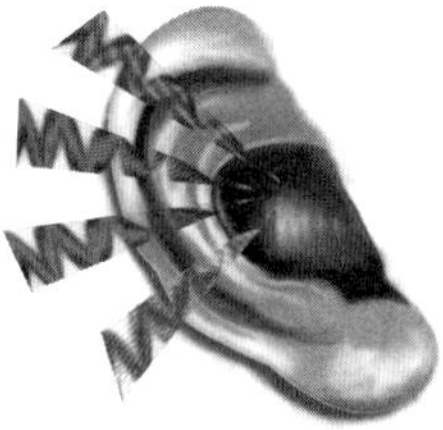

¡OYE! HEY!

Throughout this Study Sidekick, we're going to give you hints on how to pronounce Spanish words. Here are some guidelines to help you out when you use our pronunciation keys:

- *ay* sounds like the long *a* in *shake* and *bake*
- *ah* is the sound the doctor tells you to make when she shoves a stick down your throat and says, "Say ah!"
- *oh* sounds just like it does when you say *cold*
- *ee* is a long *e*, of course, like in the word *feet*
- *oo* sounds like the *oo* in *boot* and *toot*
- *bv* is a cross between a *b* and *v* (we'll talk more about this, never fear)
- *s* always sounds like the *sssss* in *snake*--it never sounds like a *z* as it sometimes does in English (like in the word *goes*)
- *italicized* syllables are *stressed*

GENERAL NOTE:

Spanish speakers don't draw vowel sounds out as long as English speakers do. When you see "ay" or any of the other vowel sounds in the pronunciation guide, make them sound more short and clipped than you do when you speak English.

See if you can figure out which letter in the Spanish alphabet doesn't appear in the English alphabet.

Spanish letter	Spanish name	approx. pronunciation
a	a	ah
b	be	bay
c	ce	say
d	de	day
e	e	ay
f	efe	ayf-fay
g	ge	hay (but make the *h* guttural and spitty, like in chutzpah)
h	hache	ah-chay
i	i	ee

j	jota	hoh-tah
k	ka	kah
l	ele	ayl-ay
m	eme	aym-ay
n	ene	ay-nay
ñ	eñe	ayn-yay
o	o	oh
p	pe	pay
q	cu	coo
r	ere	ayr-ray
s	ese	ays-ay
t	te	tay
u	u	oo
v	ve	bvay
w	doble ve	doh-blay vay
x	equis	ay-kees
y	i griega	ee gree-ay-gah
z	zeta	say-tah

If you picked ñ as the letter that appears in the Spanish alphabet but not the English alphabet, you win an all-expense-paid trip to Cybertron, home of the Transformers.™*

* With proofs of purchase from 6,500 Study Sidekicks.

Until recently, these two letter-combinations were considered actual letters in their own right and were included in the Spanish alphabet:

- **ch**
- **ll**

Ch is the letter **che.** It's pronounced just like the *ch* in the English words *chortle* and *chuckle.*

Ll is the letter **elle** and is pronounced like the *y* in the English words *yummy yam.*

> **Although** it's not considered a letter in its own right, harken to the melodic, Spanish sound of the double "rr" for a second: it sounds like a purr or a car motor. You roll it even more than a single "r."

Here's the Good News

Spanish is an easy language to pronounce. *Most letters correspond to only one sound.* Yippee! Once you learn how to pronounce each letter, you'll have Spanish pronunciation pretty much licked.

Vowels

Spanish vowels are a piece of cake. Unlike English vowels, which can make several possible sounds, there's only one correct way to pronounce Spanish vowels. All you've got to do is learn one sound per vowel and you're all set.

The Letter A

In English there are a number of ways you can pronounce the vowel *a*.

Say these words:

- *ape*
- *armpit*
- *crap*

Notice how your lips move differently when you pronounce the *a* in each word. Each *a* sounds a little different. In Spanish, *a* has only one flat sound: *ah* like in the English word *Mama* or like in the Spanish name **María**.

The Letter E

"E" is pronounced like a long *a* as in the English word table. An example in Spanish is **la cena**, which means *supper*. Pronounce it "say-nah," but don't draw out the "a" sound in either syllable.

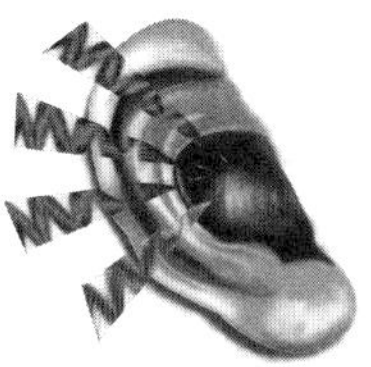

Now Hear This!

Remember, these written pronunciations are only guides. You have to listen to properly spoken Spanish to really catch on to how it should sound.

The Letter I

"I" is pronounced like a long *e* in English. It sounds kind of like the two e's in *feet*. For example, in Spanish you pronounce **el cine,** which means *movie theatre,* like this: "see-nay."

The Letter O

"O" is always pronounced like a long "o," as in the English word *total*. Examples in Spanish are **ojo,** which means *eye,* and **ojo morado,** which means *black eye*. Pronounce these words as: "oh-ho moh-rah-doh."

The Letter U

"U" is pronounced like the two o's in the English word *loop*. Remember, all these vowels should sound short and clipped, rather than drawn out. Some Spanish examples are **una trucha,** which means *a trout*, and **un eructo,** which means *a burp*. Pronounce them this way: "oo-nah troo-chah" and "oon ay-rook-toh."

COGNATES

Cognates are words in two different languages that are spelled alike and have similar or identical meanings. Cognates are your friends. Luckily, there are quite a few Spanish and English cognates. Cognates are great because they're easy to remember. They're also handy for pointing out the differences in pronunciation between Spanish and English.

For example, the word **patio** means the same thing and is spelled the same way in both Spanish and English, but the pronunciation differs between the two languages.

- In English, we say: pæh-tee-oh
- In Spanish, we say: pah-teeoh

Here are a few other cognates for you to chew on.

Colorado:

- In English we say: cah-loh-rah-doh
- In Spanish we say: coh-loh-rah-doh

¿Cómo frijoles? (Spanish for "How have you bean?")

- Unknown

Tabatha the Translator says: Notice that in English we don't pronounce the "o" the same way in the first syllable and the second syllable. In Spanish, the "o's" are pronounced the same way in both syllables. In fact, the pronunciation of "o" never changes in Spanish.

Teresa:

- In English, we say: Tuh-ree-sah
- In Spanish, we say: Tay-ray-sah

In English, the "e" in the first syllable is pronounced differently from the "e" in the second syllable. In Spanish, the "e's" are pronounced the same way in both syllables.

The Consonants

For the most part, Spanish consonants also have one sound. There are a few oddballs, however, so here are some rules to help you pronounce them correctly.

10 Quick Rules of the Tongue:

Rule Number One: The Letters "b" and "v"

In Spanish, "b" and "v" are both pronounced like a "b," kind of like we pronounce the "b" in the English word *boy*, but it's a softer, more airy sound. Let more air pass through your lips than you do when you say *boy*, but don't push the air out as much as you do when you say *very*. Try to combine the "b" and "v" sounds when you say these words:

venir / bvay-neer / *to come*

la vaca / bvah-cah / *cow*

These next "b" words should sound a bit more b-ish than the "v" words, but let more air pass through your lips than you do when you pronounce an English "b."

bueno / bway-noh / *good*

el burro / boo-rroh / *donkey*

Rule number two: the letter "c"

Spaniards have a different way of pronouncing "c."

In Latin America, when the letter "c" is placed before an "e" or an "i," it has the same sound as the English "s." This generally works the same way in English, so this is an easy rule for English speakers.

- **la cena** / say-nah / *supper*
- **el cine** / see-nay / *movie theater*
- **la ciudad** / see-yoo-dahd / *city*

In Spain, the rule is different. A "c" placed before an "e" or an "i" is pronounced as a "th" as in *thumb*. To people in Spain, it's the normal pronunciation of their language.

- **la cena** / thay-nah
- **el cine** / thee-nay
- **la ciudad** / thee-yoo-dahd

MORE ABOUT "C"

In both Spain and Latin America, when "c" comes before "a," "o," or "u," it is pronounced like the English "k." It works the same way in English. It's an easy rule for English speakers, because it makes sense instinctively.

- **la calle** / kah-yay / *street*
- **el coche** / koh-chay / *car*
- **el curso** / koor-soh / *course*

RULE NUMBER THREE: THE LETTER "G"

"G" is probably the trickiest little bugger in the alphabet, so hang in there--we'll give you the lowdown.

In Spanish, "g" sometimes sounds like a regular hard "g" in English--like *great green gobs of greasy grimy gopher guts*. The word **gracias** has a hard "g" (grah-see-ahs). When "g" is followed by "u," "a," or "o," however, it sounds just a little softer. Let a little more air pass though your throat to soften the "g" sound.

- **el garaje** / ghah-rah-hay / *garage*
- **el guante** / ghwahn-tay / *glove*
- **gordo** / ghohr-doh / *fat*

When "g" is followed by either an "e" or an "i," it sounds like the "h" in the English word *hot,* but slightly spittier and more guttural. You can hear it more than the "h" in *hot*--this scraping sound in the back of your throat isn't a regular part of the American pronunciation of English. (However, a few words we've borrowed from other languages do contain this sound: *chutzpah, aHa!, challah, Bach,* etc.)

el general / hayn-ayr-ahl / *general*

la magia / mah-hee-ah / *magic*

inteligente / een-tay-lee-hayn-tay / *intelligent*

AND THAT'S NOT ALL, FOLKS!

When "g" is following by a "ue" or "ui," the "u" is silent like in the English word *guest.* (You don't say *gwest*--or you probably don't, anyway.)

La guerra de las guitarras

lah ghay-rrah day lahs ghee-tah-rras

The war of the guitars

Occasionally, the "u" following a "g" is pronounced in Spanish words. When this is the case, there will be a little thing called a diaeresis over the "u." A diaeresis looks like a horizontal colon. It's two little dots over the letter "u," telling you that you should pronounce the "u." Again, this "g" is not silent, nor is it as hard as a hard "g" in English.

el pingüino / peen-gwee-noh / *penguin*

la cigüeña / see-gway-nyah / *stork*

Rule number four: The letter "h"

This one's so easy that it makes up for the pesky letter "g." In Spanish, "h" is always silent, as in the English word *honesty*.

la hormiga / ohr-mee-gah / *ant*

el huevo / way-bvoh / *egg*

ahora / ah-ohr-ah / *now*

Rule number five: the letter "j"

Another no-brainer -- "j" always sounds like the spitty, guttural "g." Remember how that sounds? You force air through your throat to make a spitty "h" sound.

juntos / hoon-tohs / *together*

la naranja / nah-rahn-hah / *orange*

joven / hoh-vayn / *young*

Rule number six: the letter "LL"

This letter combination used to be an official part of the Spanish alphabet. It's no longer considered a single letter, but of course it still shows up in a lot of Spanish words. It's pronounced like the letter "y" in the English word *yogurt*.

Ella lleva la llave en un bolso amarillo. / Ay-yah yay-vah lah yah-vay ayn oon bohl-soh ah-mah-ree-yoh. / *She carries the key in a yellow purse.*

Rule number seven: the letter "Ñ"

The consonant **ñ** is pronounced like "ny" in the word *canyon*. The little squiggly thing over the "n" is called a tilde. The tilde lets you know that you should say "ny" instead of "n."

el año / ah-nyoh / *year*

el niño / nee-nyoh / *little boy*

la uña / oo-nyah / *fingernail*

Rule number eight: the letter "Q"

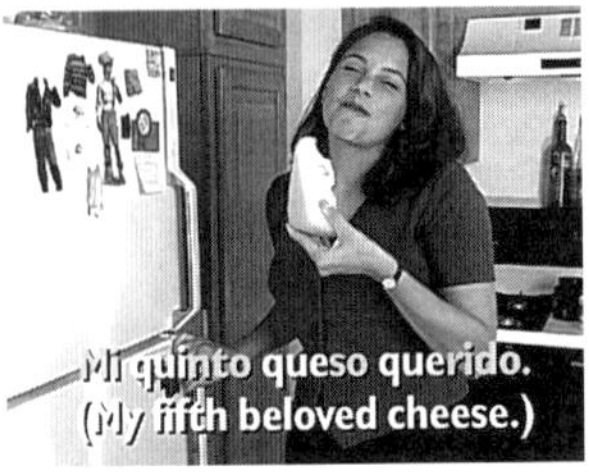

"Q" is pronounced like the "k" in *kitchen*. Easy peasy schmeesy. In Spanish, "q" is always followed by "ue" or "ui," and the "u" is always silent.

Mi quinto queso querido / mee keen-toh kay-soh kay-ree-doh / *My fifth beloved cheese*

Rule number nine: the letter "RR"

You might have to do some tongue exercises to get used to this one. "Rr" is a rolled "r," so it sounds like a purr or a car motor.

TIP OF THE TONGUE: Think of the *r* sound in Spanish like the sound of the two *t*'s in English when you say *butter*, *batter*, or *ladder*. It's just a quick flap of your tongue against your palate. That's how you pronounce the *r* sound in Spanish words like *para*, *quiero*, or *hablar*. /pah-rah/ /kee-yeh-roh/ /ah-blahr/

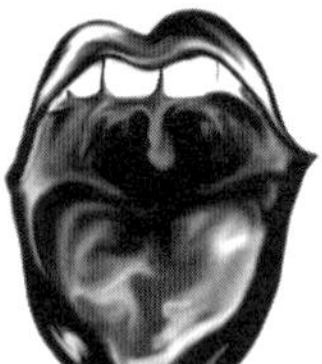

el carro - *car*

el burro - *donkey*

DON'T FORGET that all *r's* are rolled or trilled. The double *rr* is just rolled twice as much.

Here's a tongue twister with lots of **rr**'s to roll.

We dare you to say it ten times fast.

El carro y el ferrocarril corren rápido.

The car and the train go fast.

Good work, troopers! Here's another one. You have to trill the **r**'s at the beginnings of these words. Try to do it without spitting this time.

Rubén riñe con una rata en Río.

Ruben quarrels with a rat in Rio.

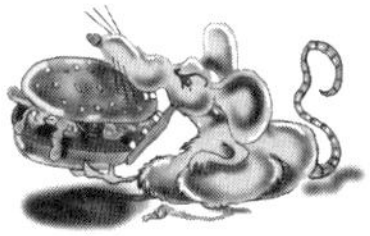

Rule Number Ten: The Letter "z"

"Z" is another letter that is pronounced differently in Latin America than in Spain.

In Latin America, "z" is pronounced like an "s" in English.

El zapato del Zorro está en el azúcar. / Ayl sah-pah-toh dayl Sorr-oh ays-tah ayn ayl ah-soo-kahr / *Zorro's shoe is in the sugar.*

Spaniards pronounce "z" the same way they do a "c" that comes before an "e" or an "i." They make "z" sound like the "th" in the word *thumb.*

El zapato del Zorro está en el azúcar. / Ayl thah-pah-toh dayl Thorr-oh ays-tah ayn ayl ah-thoo-kahr / *Zorro's shoe is in the sugar.*

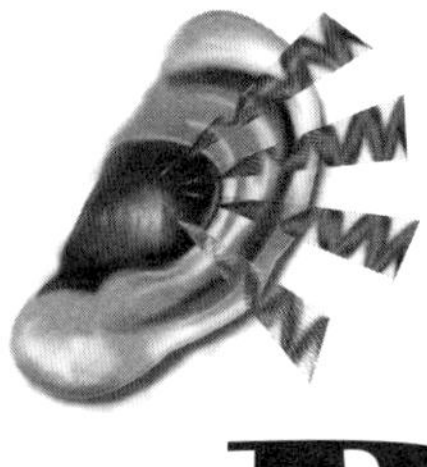

Now Hear This:

The English pronunciation of "z" like in *zebra* is never used in Spanish.

REMEMBER: No Zebras! no zest! No zoo!

Practice saying these sentences. After you say them, check the pronunciation guide on the next page to see if you pronounced them correctly. Don't peek at the guide until you try to say each sentence at least a couple of times!

Mi mamá me ama.
My mother loves me.

Teresa tiene una tetera de Nepal.
Teresa has a teapot from Nepal.

Viviana visita la India.
Vivian visits India.

Yo como cocos con Carlos.
I eat coconuts with Carlos.

Lucía lucha por la justicia humana.
Lucia struggles for human justice.

We've italicized the syllables that should be stressed.

- **Mi mamá me ama.** / Mee mah-*mah* may *ah*-mah

- **Teresa tiene una tetera de Nepal.** /
  Tay-*ray*-sah *teeay*-nay *oo*-nah tay-*tay*-rah day Nay-*pahl*

- **Yo como cocos con Carlos.** /
  Yoh *coh*-moh *coh*-cohs cohn *Cahr*-lohs

- **Viviana visita la India.** /
  Bvee-bvee-*ah*-nah bvee-*see*-tah lah *Een*-dee-ah

- **Lucía lucha por la justicia humana.** /
  Loo-*see*-ah *loo*-chah pohr lah hoos-*tee*-see-ah hoo-*mah*-nah

Diphthongs

A **diphthong** is a combination of two vowels pronounced as one sound and one syllable. Diphthongs can be a combination of the two vowels that are considered "weak vowels":

- i
- u

They can also be one of the weak vowels paired with one of the "strong vowels":

- a
- e
- o

Diphthongs, which are called **diptongos** in Spanish, blend two vowel sounds into a single sound. We can use the cognate **patio** again as an example:

In English, we make "patio" a three syllable word: pæh-tee-oh.

In Spanish, the "i" and the "o" blend together into one sound, making **el patio** a two-syllable word: pah-teeoh.

Here are some more examples of Spanish **diptongos.**

- **el aguacate** (*avocado*)

The "u" and the "a" blend to make the sound "wah": ah-gwah-*cah*-tay

el piano (guess what, it means *piano*)

The "i" and the "a" blend to make the sound "eeyah," which is said as a single syllable: *peeyah*-noh

siete (the number *seven*)

The "i" and the "e" blend to make the sound "eeyay" which, again, is said as a single syllable: seeyay-tay

SECTION B: CAPITALIZATION AND ACCENTS

Vocabulary

el modo - *manner/ way*

americano(a) - *American*

el modo americano - *American way*

el café - *coffee*

colombiano(a) - *Colombian*

café colombiano - *Colombian coffee*

loco(a) - *lunatic, crazy*

el presidente - *President*

el nombre - *name*

la rosa - *rose*

el sombrero - *hat*

nuevo(a) - *new*

CAPITALIZATION

The rules of capitalization in Spanish are a bit different from the rules in English. They aren't hard, but you do have to learn them, since a lot of words that are capitalized in English are not capitalized in Spanish.

Just think how strange it would look to you if someone wrote you a letter dated monday, march 3rd--you'd wonder if they forgot to eat their Frosted Sugar Chocopops that morning. For the same reason, it's important to learn how to capitalize the Spanish way.

1. Days and Months

The names of the days of the week and the names of the months are written with lowercase letters in Spanish. They are not capitalized as they are in English.

- **February** / *febrero*
- **March** / *marzo*
- **Monday** /*lunes*
- **Tuesday** / *martes*

Turn to the Video Notes for *The Salsa-riffic World of Spanish Part 2* for a complete listing of the days and months in Spanish!

2. The Pronoun "Yo"

Yo is the Spanish pronoun that means *I*. Unless **yo** is the first word of a sentence, it is not capitalized.

- English: *He thinks that I am a dirty rat.*
- Spanish: **Él cree que yo soy una rata asquerosa.**

3. Proper Adjectives and Nouns

Proper adjectives refer to a specific quality and proper nouns refer to a specific person, place, or thing. We generally capitalize them in English, but they are not capitalized in Spanish.

Proper Adjectives

In the following example, *American* is a proper adjective modifying the noun *way*. It's considered "proper" because it refers to a specific group. Because it's a proper adjective, *American* is capitalized in English. The Spanish word for *American* is **americano**, and is *not* capitalized.

- English: *The American way*
- Spanish: **El modo americano**

Notice that **the noun modo, which means *way* or *method*, goes before the proper adjective americano. This is the way adjectives are placed in Spanish. See SOME GRAMMATICAL STUFF, Section A, in *The Salsa-riffic World of Spanish Part 2* for more details on the placement of Spanish adjectives.**

In English, you capitalize *Colombian* when you write *Colombian coffee* because *Colombian* is a proper adjective. However, you don't capitalize it in Spanish.

- English: *Colombian coffee*
- Spanish: **café colombiano**

4. Proper Nouns

American can also be used as a noun. The next example uses *American* as a proper noun modified by the adjective *lunatic*.

- English: *the lunatic American*
- Spanish: **el americano loco**

In the phrase *the lunatic American, lunatic* is an adjective that, by itself, could refer to any crazy person, regardless of race, creed, nationality, or favorite variety of cheese. *Lunatic* is not specific. It is not a proper adjective, so it is not capitalized in either language. *American* is the word that gets specific. In this phrase it is a proper noun; so according to the English rules, it must be capitalized. The Spanish version, **americano**, does not get capitalized because in Spanish you don't capitalize proper nouns.

WAIT!
THERE'S MORE!
Don't go off half-cocked!

There's an exception to this rule--just one easy little exception. In Spanish, as in English, proper nouns and adjectives are capitalized when they're part of a name.

- English: *United States of America*
- Spanish: **Estados Unidos de América**

All the words are capitalized in both languages because they are part of a name. Puny prepositions like **de** (*of*) don't get capitalized in English or Spanish.

5. The Beginning of a Sentence

In Spanish, like in English, you use capital letters at the beginning of a sentence. And that's all we have to say about that.

6. Names

Capitalize all proper names, such as people's names, the names of cities, the names of countries, companies, dogs, streets, and brands of cheese. This is true in both Spanish and English. If it's a name, capitalize it.

7. People's Titles

People's titles are capitalized in English, but not in Spanish.

- English: *President Nixon*
- Spanish: **el presidente Nixon**

In English, we capitalize the word *president* when we write *President Nixon*, because it's part of his title. However, don't capitalize the Spanish equivalent, **presidente**. *Nixon* is capitalized in both languages because it's a name.

Sheesh, good thing you know English already! Ee gads!

8. Book Titles

Spanish and English rules differ when it comes to capitalizing book titles. In Spanish, you *only* capitalize the first word of a book title. *Always*. In English, we capitalize all the words except puny prepositions and so on--of course, we do capitalize those too, if they are the first word in a title. Right on.

- English: *The Name of the Rose*
- Spanish: **El nombre de la rosa**

BUT BUT BUT...

There is an exception to this rule. If the book title contains a proper name, like the name of a person or a country, you capitalize the name. That's easy to remember, because you **ALWAYS CAPITALIZE NAMES.**

- English: *Curious George Buys a New Hat*
- Spanish: **Curious George compra un sombrero nuevo**

Even in Spanish you have to capitalize **George**, because it's a name. Granted, it's the name of a monkey, but it's a name nonetheless.

Accents

Think of written accents like they're letters in a word. If you don't put an accent where there ought to be one, you're spelling the word incorrectly. There are two primary purposes for the written accents on Spanish words:

- To indicate an irregular stress pattern in a word
- To differentiate between two words that are spelled the same way but have different meanings

There are rules in Spanish that dictate which syllable is supposed to be stressed in the pronunciation of a word. You'll probably learn about these rules in more advanced Spanish classes. For now, just remember that if the word doesn't follow the regular rules for stressed syllables, you have to add an accent mark to indicate the irregularly stressed syllable.

Sometimes accents indicate a difference in meaning rather than an irregularity in stress pattern. For example, the Spanish word **solo** without an accent means *alone*. The word **sólo** with an accent means *only*. Both words are pronounced exactly the same way. The accent on **sólo** indicates the difference in meaning. Here's another example:

- **se** (with no accent) = a reflexive pronoun
- **sé** (with an accent) = a verb that means *I know*

Both words are pronounced exactly the same way, but the accent mark indicates a difference in meaning.

You'll learn more about reflexive pronouns in more advanced Spanish classes. For now, cool your jets and just learn about accents and what they can do for you.

Summary

- In Spanish, the names of the days of the week and the names of the months are written with lowercase letters.

- Don't capitalize the pronoun **yo**.

- Don't capitalize proper nouns or adjectives unless they are part of a proper name.

- Capitalize all proper names, including people's names, the names of countries, and the names of cities.

- Don't capitalize people's titles (like *president, doctor, judge, gastroenterologist*).

- Capitalize only the first word of a book title, unless the title contains a proper name that must be capitalized.

Accents ARE PART OF HOW A WORD IS SPELLED. **MEMORIZE THEM** ALONG WITH THE LETTERS OF A WORD!

- Accents indicate one of two things: an irregular stress pattern or a difference in meaning.

SECTION C: THE NUMBERS 0 TO 99

Vocabulary

el dinero - *money*

el pato - *duck*

los abogados - *lawyers*

el dentista - *dentist*

las plantas - *plants*

el tostador - *toaster*

las tazas - *cups*

las manzanas - *apples*

los escritores - *writers*

los árboles - *trees*

The Numbers 1 Through 10

0 **cero** *zero* — **cero puntos** *zero points*

1 **uno** *one* — **un pato** *one duck*

2 **dos** *two* — **dos abogados** *two lawyers*

3 **tres** *three* — **tres dentistas** *three dentists*

	4	**cuatro** *four*	**cuatro plantas** *four plants*
	5	**cinco** *five*	**cinco tostadores** *five toasters*
	6	**seis** *six*	**seis tazas** *six cups*
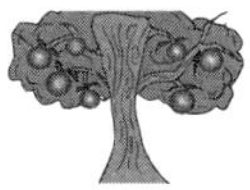	7	**siete** *seven*	**siete naranjas** *seven oranges*
	8	**ocho** *eight*	**ocho manzanas** *eight apples*
	9	**nueve** *nine*	**nueve escritores** *nine writers*
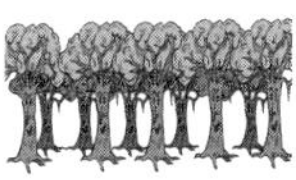	10	**diez** *ten*	**diez árboles** *ten trees*

DID YOU NOTICE?

In Spanish, the number *one* is **uno**, but when we used **uno** with the noun **pato**, **uno** became **un**. That's because when you use the number *one* along with a noun, you have to make the number match in gender with the noun it's paired with. We go into the details of nouns and gender in **Section A** of **Articles and Pronouns**. For now, just consider this: If a noun ends in "o," it's usually considered masculine and if it ends in "a," it's probably considered feminine.

- When you want to use the number *one* (**uno**) *before a masculine noun*, use the form **un**.

- When you use the number one (**uno**) *with a feminine noun*, use the form **una**. The "a" at the end of **una** matches the feminine gender of your noun.

For example, the noun **mesa**, which means *table*, is feminine and ends in "a." To say *one table*, say **una mesa**.

IN A NUTSHELL

There are **3 ways** to say the number ***one***:

1. uno

2. un

3. una

PICK the one you need **according** to what you're **DESCRIBING.**

1. If you're just counting, say **uno**.

2. If you're using the number *one* as an adjective modifying a masculine noun, say **un**.

3. If you are using it to modify a feminine noun, say **una**.

The Numbers 11-20

Here are they are. Memorize 'em, baby:

11	**once**	*eleven*
12	**doce**	*twelve*
13	**trece**	*thirteen*
14	**catorce**	*fourteen*
15	**quince**	*fifteen*
16	**dieciséis**	*sixteen*
17	**diecisiete**	*seventeen*
18	**dieciocho**	*eighteen*
19	**diecinueve**	*nineteen*
20	**veinte**	*twenty*

The Numbers 20-99

To learn the numbers from 20 to 99, start with the multiples of ten. The numbers in between work like they do in English--just tack on the single-digit number.

Now let's take a look at the numbers between twenty and twenty-nine:

Word of Mouth:

You should be aware that there's another way to write the numbers between 16 and 29. You can write these numbers as three words instead of one. This spelled-out form follows the same convention as numbers larger than thirty: diez y seis, diez y siete, diez y ocho, diez y nueve...viente y ocho, veinte y nueve.

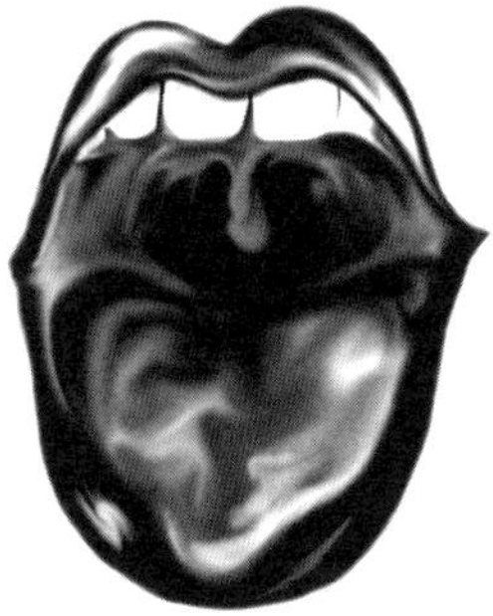

20	**veinte**	*twenty*
21	**veintiuno**	*twenty-one*
22	**veintidós**	*twenty-two*
23	**veintitrés**	*twenty-three*
24	**veinticuatro**	*twenty-four*
25	**veinticinco**	*twenty-five*

26	**veintiséis**	*twenty-six*
27	**veintisiete**	*twenty-seven*
28	**veintiocho**	*twenty-eight*
29	**veintinueve**	*twenty-nine*

The Spanish word for 30 is treinta.

30	**treinta**	*thirty*
31	**treinta y uno**	*thirty-one*
38	**treinta y ocho**	*thirty-eight*
39	**treinta y nueve**	*thirty-nine*

The y between the multiple of ten and the single digit means *and*. Here are the rest of the multiples of ten:

40	**cuarenta**	*forty*
50	**cincuenta**	*fifty*
60	**sesenta**	*sixty*
70	**setenta**	*seventy*
80	**ochenta**	*eighty*
90	**noventa**	*ninety*

So much for the numbers in this video. If you want to learn how to count past 99, you've gotta take a look at *The Salsa-riffic World of Spanish Part 2.*

SECTION D: HONEY, WE NEED TO TALK

If you're going to speak to people in Spanish, you have to know how to be polite. These pleasantries are just something you have to know in any language. You can't run up to a Spanish speaker and say, "Quit speakin' your moonman language and tell me where I can find a snow cone!" You have to be polite and genteel, and we're here to tell you how to do that.

VOCABULARY

la clase - *class*

¿A dónde vas? - *Where are you going?*

la historia - *history*

también - *also*

perdedor - *loser*

Now let's use some of these invaluable phrases. Here's a classic conversation between two friends who run into each other on campus. Be proper and polite like these two and your mother will be very proud of you.

When walking through a melon patch, don't adjust your sandals.

- Chinese proverb

These commonly-used phrases are helpful to know. For now, just memorize them like vocabulary words. As you learn more Spanish, you'll learn how they work grammatically.

tengo prisa - *I'm in a hurry*

nos vemos - *see you later*

está bien - *okay; it's okay*

¿Qué haces hoy? - *What are you doing today?*

¡Qué sorpresa! - *What a surprise!*

Greetings

Here are three ways to greet people. These phrases work in both formal and informal situations. In other words, it's okay to use these greetings with friends and family, as well as people you don't know very well, don't know at all, or to whom you need to show respect. A useful thing about these greetings is that you can use them when you first see someone *or* when you are ready to leave 'em behind in the dust.

- **Buenos días** - *Good morning*
- **Buenas tardes** - *Good afternoon*
- **Buenas noches** - *Good night*

Here are some less formal greetings. You're more likely to use these with your friends and family.

¡Hola! - *Hi!*

¿Cómo estás? - *How are you?*

¿Qué tal? - *How are you?*

¿Cómo te va? - *How is it going?*

Bien, gracias. ¿Y tú? - *Fine, thank you. And you?*

No muy bien. ¿Y tú? - *Not very well. And you?*

Así, así. - *So-so.*

adiós - *goodbye*

hasta luego - *see you later*

cíao - *goodbye*

nos vemos - *see you later*

Punctuation

You probably noticed the upside-down question marks in some of the phrases above. In Spanish, questions have upside-down question marks at the beginning of the question and right-side-up ones at the end. Cool stuff, eh? Exclamation points work the same way: one upside-down at the beginning of the phrase or sentence, and one right-side-up at the end.

> **Actually**
> PERIODS ARE WRITTEN UPSIDE-DOWN IN SPANISH. **You just can't tell** BECAUSE A PERIOD IS TINY AND ROUND.

MARGARITA:
"Buenos días, Roberto."
(Good morning, Roberto.)

ROBERTO:
"Buenos días, Margarita. ¿Cómo estás?"
(Good morning, Margarita. How are you?)

MARGARITA:
"Muy bien, gracias. ¿Y tú?"
(Very well, thank you. And you?)

ROBERTO:
"Así, así."
(So-so.)

MARGARITA:
"¿A dónde vas?"
(Where are you going?)

ROBERTO:
"A mi clase de historia."
(To my history class.)

MARGARITA:
"Yo también voy a clase."
(I'm going to class, too.)

ROBERTO:
"Bueno, tengo prisa. Nos vemos."
(Well, I'm in a rush. I'll see you.)

MARGARITA:
"Está bien, hasta luego."
(Okay. See you later.)

QUIZ I

1) Spell these words out loud to practice the letters of the Spanish alphabet.

a. el regalo: _ _ _ _ _ _

b. la ciudad: _ _ _ _ _ _

2) Write the English equivalents of these Spanish words.

a. el general: ____________________

b. el piano: ____________________

3) What do you call the little dots (¨) that sometimes appear over the vowel *u*?

a. un diptongo

b. una diéresis

c. un acento

4) Capitalize the following Spanish expressions where appropriate.

a. la azúcar cubana: __________ ____________

b. el americano gordo:______________________

5) Which of these statements is true?

a. In Spanish we use accents to indicate which syllable should be stressed in the pronunciation of a word.

b. Accents have nothing to do with a difference in meaning.

c. Accents are unrelated to the spelling of Spanish words.

6) Write out the solutions to these math problems in Spanish.

a. 8 + 7 = ____________________

b. 15 + 6 = ____________________

c. 25 + 14 = ____________________

d. 33 + 27 = ____________________

e. 44 + 42 = ____________________

7) Match these English words with their Spanish equivalents.

a. la cena	**1.** cheese
b. bonito	**2.** thank you
c. el ojo	**3.** eye
d. el coche	**4.** dinner
e. gracias	**5.** fast
f. la cigüeña	**6.** hat
g. rápido	**7.** beautiful
h. el queso	**8.** car
i. el sombrero	**9.** name
j. el nombre	**10.** stork

8) Respond to these people's greetings.

a. ¡Hola! ____________________

b. ¿Cómo estás? ____________________

c. ¿Qué tal? ____________________

d. ¿Cómo te va? ____________________

e. ¡Nos vemos! ____________________

9) Translate these English phrases into Spanish. (Check the glossary if you need a hint.)

a. What a surprise! ____________________

b. Hi! ____________________

c. Loser!____________________

d. Where are you going?

____

e. How are you?

____

SECTION A: ARTICLES

Vocabulary

la mesa - *table*

That's all! Now let's learn about SEX. Whoopee!

Gender with Nouns and Adjectives

In Spanish, just about everything is a girl or a boy. Okay, that sounds silly, but here's what we mean. Nouns and pronouns--as well as the adjectives and articles that modify them--all express gender. Inanimate objects like tables, rocks, and nosehair clippers are all considered either masculine or feminine. Of course, there are pesky exceptions, but here are some general guidelines.

- If a Spanish noun ends in "a," it's considered a feminine noun. Any adjectives you use to modify it should be feminine and end in "a."

If a noun ends in "o," it's considered a masculine noun, and any adjectives you use to modify it should be masculine and end in "o."

Articles: Definite / Indefinite

What the Heck Are Articles?

Articles are considered adjectives because they tell you something about the nouns they modify. The English articles are those useful little words *a*, *an*, and *the*.

Definite Articles

Definite articles *specify* which thing or person you're talking about. The only definite article in English is *the*. When you refer to *the* sticky spot on the floor, you're referring to a *specific* sticky spot, and not just any old puddle of goo.

Indefinite Articles

Indefinite articles are more general and don't refer to one *specific* thing. The English indefinite articles are *a*, *an*, and *the* plural indefinite article is *some*. If you refer to *a* sticky spot on the floor, you're not pointing out one spot in particular. You could be talking about any sticky spot. That's what makes indefinite articles indefinite.

Spanish Definite Articles

- el
- los
- la
- las

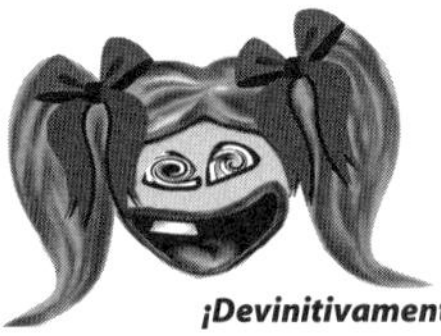

¡Devinitivamente!

The four Spanish definite articles describe the nouns they modify with more detail than *the* does in English. Spanish definite articles tell you whether the nouns they modify are masculine or feminine, singular or plural.

- Use **el** with a singular masculine noun

  el carro - *the car*

You may have noticed various articles floating around this workbook and in the video—that's because it's helpful to **learn the definite article at the same time as you learn a new word,** so you'll always remember that they go **TOGETHER.**

NOTE: There is a variety of ways to say *car* in Spanish, depending on which country you're in. Latin Americans often say **el carro** or **el auto**, while Spaniards say **el coche**.

- Use **los** with a plural masculine noun

los carros - *the cars*

- Use **la** with a singular feminine noun

la mesa - *the table*

- Use **las** with a plural feminine noun

las mesas - *the tables*

Spanish Indefinite Articles

- **un** - **unos**
- **una** - **unas**

In Spanish, there are four indefinite articles that tell a bit more about the nouns they modify than their English counterparts.

Just like definite articles, indefinite articles tell you if the nouns they modify are masculine or feminine, singular or plural.

Use **un** with a singular masculine noun

un carro - *a car*

Use **unos** with a plural masculine noun

unos carros - *some cars*

Use **una** with a singular feminine noun

una mesa - *a table*

Use **unas** with a plural feminine noun

unas mesas - *some tables*

SUMMARY

In Spanish, inanimate objects and all other nouns are considered either masculine or feminine.

Usually, if a word ends in "a" it's feminine, and if it ends in "o" it's masculine.

It is fun being in the same decade with you.

- Franklin Delano Roosevelt in a letter to Winston Churchill, 1942

Adjectives and articles that modify nouns have to correspond in gender and number with the nouns they're modifying.

Articles are little words like *a* and *the* that tell you something about the word that follows them. Definite articles point out specific things, and indefinite articles are nonspecific.

When you use a Spanish definite article or indefinite article, make sure that it matches your noun in gender and number.

SECTION B: PRONOUNS

A pronoun is a word that takes the place of a noun. We use them so we don't have to repeat the same nouns over and over again. This makes our speech more efficient. Otherwise, we'd sound like this:

Tanya got up late and missed the bus. Tanya didn't have enough money for a taxi. Tanya walked. Tanya walked all the way to work. Tanya bought donuts with her last dollar. Eating donuts cheered Tanya up. Tanya especially likes jelly-filled donuts, creme-filled donuts, and chocolate-covered donuts.

Woo, gender benders.

You

In English, the pronoun *you* has many uses. It can be either singular or plural, and it can refer to anyone, young or old, friend or stranger.

There are five (count 'em) *five* Spanish pronouns that mean *you.*

- **tú**
- **usted**
- **ustedes**
- **vosotros**
- **vosotras**

We will only focus on three ways to say *you*: **tú, usted,** and **ustedes.** These three are used in all Spanish-speaking countries. However, we will briefly go over the pronouns **vosotros** and **vosotras,** which are only used in Spain.

Tú

"Tú! Tú! Tú!"

Use the singular pronoun **tú** to address a person who is your peer. In other words, **tú** refers to a person whom you know well and who is not a lot older or in a higher position than you. **Tú** can also refer to your equal, someone who is younger than you, or someone who has less status than you.

Usted

Use **usted** when you refer to someone whom you don't know or don't know very well, or with someone who is older or holds a higher position than you. You would probably refer to your boss or your grandmother as **usted**. You would definitely call a new acquaintance **usted** until you got to know her better. If you're ever in doubt about whether to use **tú** or **usted**, use **usted** to be safe.

Ustedes

This plural pronoun is used differently in Latin America and Spain. In Latin America, **ustedes** is used in any situation that calls for a plural pronoun that means *you*. (In other words, it means *you guys* or *y'all*.) If you're addressing a group directly, call them **ustedes**. **Ustedes** is also used in Spain, but like **usted**, it's considered a formal pronoun, so it's used to address a group of strangers or people with higher status than the speaker.

"Ustedes!"

Take note:

Usted is often abbreviated as **Ud.** and **ustedes** is often abbreviated as **Uds.** These abbreviations are similar to the English abbreviations for *Mister (Mr.)* and *Missus (Mrs.)* in English. When you write out the word **usted** or **ustedes**, use a lowercase "u" unless, of course, it's the first word in a sentence. When you abbreviate the words, use upper case **u's**, whether they are at the beginning of the sentence or not.

Vosotros/Vosotras

These are the informal plural pronouns for *you* and are only used in Spain. Unlike in Latin America, where **ustedes** is used in any situation (formal or informal) that calls for a plural pronoun that means *you*, **ustedes** is used only for formal situations in Spain. **Vosotros** and **vosotras** are used in informal situations.

- Use **vosotros** when you address a group of men or a group of both men and women.

- Use **vosotras** to address a group of women as *you*.

It's that gender thing again. But you don't have to consider gender when you use **ustedes.** It works when you refer to a group of men, women, or both.

Now that we've conquered the many evil faces of "YOU," let us turn our swords to the other pronouns...

Yo

Yo is the Spanish pronoun for *I*. Refer to yourself as **yo** whether you're male or female.

Nosotros/Nosotras

These are the pronouns that mean *we*. You can tell by the two forms (one with an "a" and one with an "o"), that you have to consider gender when you want to say *we* in Spanish.

- If you're a woman in a group of women, refer to yourselves as **nosotras**.
- If you are a man in a group of men, refer to yourselves as **nosotros**.
- If you're in a group of of both men and women, use **nosotros**, the masculine form.

Él/Ella

Él is the Spanish word for *he*. It is the third-person singular masculine pronoun.

> **"ÉL"** is spelled just like the article **el**, except there's an accent over the "e." The accent lets you know that this **él** is the pronoun *he* rather than the article *the*. This is one of those cases where the accent on a word is essential to its meaning.

The Spanish word for *she* is **ella**. It is the third-person singular feminine pronoun.

Ellos/Ellas

There are two third-person, plural pronouns in Spanish. One is masculine and the other is feminine.

- When you refer to a group of men or a group of both men and women, call them **ellos**.

- When you refer to a group of women, call them **ellas**.

SUMMARY

- The pronoun **yo** works for both men and women.

- Two pronouns mean *you* in the singular form and can be used for men or women: **tú** (informal) and **usted** (formal).

- *We* is either **nosotros** or **nosotras**, depending on the company you're keeping.

- The most commonly-used plural form of *you* is **ustedes. Ustedes** works with groups of men, women, and mixed groups.

QUIZ II

> A team is a team is a team.
> Shakespeare said that many times.
>
> - Dan Devine, football coach

1) Write the appropriate definite article for each of these Spanish words.

a. __ mesa

b. __ carro

c. __ pato

d. __ tazas

e. __ plantas

2) Write the indefinite article for each of these Spanish words.

a. __ cena

b. __ ojo

c. __ trucha

d. __ burro

e. __ guantes

3) Write the plural form of these articles and words:

a. el cine: ___ ________________

b. una vaca: ___ ________________

c. un carro: ___ ________________

d. la guerra: ___ ________________

e. un año: ___ ________________

4) Which group of words *only* contains words of *one gender* (masculine or feminine)?

- **a.** yo, nosotras, vosotros, ustedes, ella
- **b.** usted, ellos, ustedes, vosotras
- **c.** él, nosotros, vosotros, ellos

5) Which is the singular Spanish pronoun you would use to address an old pal?

- **a.** tú
- **b.** usted
- **c.** yo

6) Which of these statements is false?

- **a.** There are five Spanish pronouns that mean *you*.
- **b.** The pronoun *I* in Spanish is always capitalized.
- **c.** **Nosotros/nosotras** are the Spanish pronouns for *we*.

7) For each of these pronouns, write the equivalent pronoun of opposite gender. (For example, if the word is masculine, fill in its feminine counterpart, and vice versa.)

a. nosotras: ______________

b. él: ______________

c. ellas: ______________

d. vosotros: ______________

Fall is my favorite season in Los Angeles, watching the birds change color and fall from the trees.

- David Letterman

THE VERBS "SER" AND "ESTAR"

SECTION A: USING THE VERB "SER"

Vocabulary

lo siento - *I am sorry*
el perro - *dog*
bonito(a) - *pretty*
las sillas - *chairs*
antiguo(a) - *antique*
guapo(a) - *handsome*
la hija - *daughter*

un(a) desordenado(a)- *a slob*
un caballo - *a horse*
horrible - *horrible*
una panadería - *a bakery*
las galletas - *cookies*
gratis - *free*

Differences Between "Ser" and "Estar"

In Spanish, there are two verbs that mean *to be*: **ser** and **estar**. These two verbs have slightly different meanings and uses.

There are certain conditions that call for the verb **ser** rather than the verb **estar**, although they both mean *to be*. In other words, we use the two forms to express different conditions. In a very general sense, **ser** usually refers to a permanent condition and **estar** usually refers to a variable or temporary condition.

The Verb "Ser"

Conjugating "Ser"

When you go through all the forms of a verb, it is called "conjugating" the verb. In Spanish, most verbs are predictable and pretty easy to conjugate. However, there are certain verbs with unpredictable conjugations. These verbs are called irregular verbs. **Ser** is an irregular verb, so you just have to memorize its forms.

For those of you who haven't seen a verb conjugation since elementary school, here's the conjugation of the English verb *to be*.

TO BE

I AM

you ARE

he/she IS

we ARE

you ARE

they ARE

Did that refresh your memory?

Brrr, CHILLY!

Here's the conjugation of the Spanish verb **ser.**

SER

yo SOY

tú ERES

él/ella/usted ES

nosotros/nosotras SOMOS

ellos/ellas/ustedes SON

Using "Ser" to Express Your Place of Origin

We mentioned earlier that you often use **ser** when you're talking about a permanent or relatively permanent situation. The place where you come from falls into that category--it's considered a permanent thing and calls for the verb **ser.**

Examples

1. Spanish: **Yo soy de los Estados Unidos.**

   English: *I am from the United States.*

Here's How the Sentence Works:

- **yo** means *I*
- **soy** means *am*
- **de** means *from*
- **los** is the correct form of the article *the* to go along with **Estados Unidos**
- **Estados Unidos** means *United States*

2. Soy de México.

I am from Mexico.

Notice that in this example we did not need to use a pronoun with **soy**. **Soy** implies the pronoun *I* all by itself, since there is no other pronoun that can go with **soy**.

3. Ella es de Bogotá, Colombia.

She is from Bogota, Colombia.

Ella is the pronoun that means *she*. We need the pronoun in this sentence because **es**, the third-person singular form of **ser**, can be used with **ella**, **él**, or **usted**. Unless it's obvious whom you're talking about, you have to use a pronoun with third-person singular verb forms like **es**.

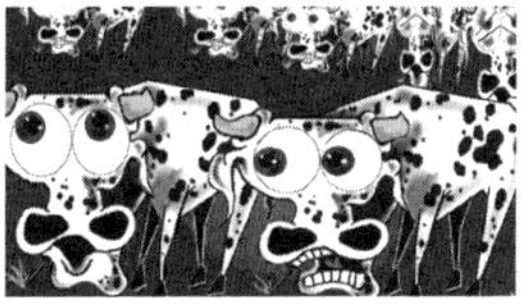

4. *Somos de Argentina.*

We are from Argentina.

In this example we didn't use a pronoun because **somos** is only used with **nosotros**, so **nosotros** is implied by the verb.

These are verb forms you can use without a pronoun:

- **the first-person singular and plural forms (yo and nosotros / nosotras)**
- **the second-person informal (tú) form**

All other verb forms require a pronoun unless it's obvious to whom the speaker is referring. This is true for any Spanish verb. (Later on in advanced Spanish classes, you'll learn more about when you have to use pronouns with conjugated verbs.)

Using "Ser" to Describe Permanent Characteristics

Use **ser** to describe the permanent characteristics of a person, place, or thing. For example, beauty is considered a permanent characteristic.

Examples

1. El perro es bonito.

The dog is beautiful.

Here's How the Sentence Works:

- The article **el** means *the*, and it matches the singular, masculine subject, **perro**.
- **Perro** means *dog*.
- **Es** is the the third-person singular form of the verb **ser**. It matches the third-person singular noun **perro**.
- **Bonito** is an adjective that means *beautiful*. It is the masculine singular form (ending in "o") because it also has to match **perro**, which is masculine and singular.

If we were talking about a girl dog, the sentence would go like this:

La perra es bonita. - *The dog is beautiful.*

- The article **la** is feminine to go along with **perra**, which means *female dog*.

- The verb **es** is the same as in the boy dog example, because **es** works for any third-person singular subject, masculine or feminine.
- The adjective **bonita** ends with an "a," because it's modifying a feminine subject, **perra**.

All the parts match. In this case, they are all singular and/or feminine.

2. Las sillas son antiguas.

The chairs are antiques.

Here's how the sentence works:

- Use the verb **ser** because the chairs aren't going to get any younger. They will be antiques until they rot; this is a permanent condition.

- **Las** is feminine and plural to match the feminine plural subject **sillas.**
- **Son** is the third-person plural form of **ser** which matches **sillas.**
- **Antiguas** is feminine and plural.

Notice that the verb and all the adjectives have to match in gender and number with the subject of the sentence. Putting together a Spanish sentence is like putting together a puzzle. All the pieces have to match up or it doesn't work.

Here are some more cases that call for the verb **ser.**

3. Soy guapo.

I am handsome.

4. Hija, eres una desordenada.

Daughter, you are a slob.

5. Somos horribles!

We are horrible!

6. **¡Bienvenidos a la Panadería de Fernando! ¡Las galletas son gratis!**

Welcome to Fernando's Bakery! The cookies are free!

SECTION B: USING ESTAR

Vocabulary

cansado(a) - *tired*

el loco - *the fool*

el pollo - *chicken*

la cocina - *kitchen*

la luna - *the moon*

feliz - *happy*

triste - *sad*

loco(a) - *crazy*

confundido(a) - *confused*

borracho(a) - *drunk*

The Conjugation of "Estar"

Estar is called an **-ar** verb because it ends in "ar." There are also **-er** and **-ir** verbs, which we'll talk more about in *The Salsa-riffic World of Spanish Part 2.* Notice as we go through the conjugation of **estar** that it's the "ar" at the end of the verb that changes. The **e-s-t,** which is the root of the verb, remains the same.

I don't have a photograph, but you can have my footprints. They're upstairs in my socks.

- Groucho Marx

yo estoy

tú estás

él/ella/usted está

nosotros/nosotras estamos

ellos/ellas/ustedes están

¡OYE! HEY!

"Estás," está," and "están" must have accents, or they are spelled incorrectly. In fact, if you write "esta" or "estas" without an accent, they are not forms of the verb "estar," they mean something entirely different--which you'll learn about in *The Salsa-riffic World of Spanish Part 2.*

Using "Estar"

You will generally use **estar** to describe the characteristics of a person, place, or thing if these characteristics are *subject to change.*

Examples

1. Él está cansado.

He is tired.

Even though he looks like he's pulled three consecutive all-nighters, this guy won't be tired forever, so we'll use **estar** to describe his condition. **Está** is the third-person singular form of the verb that matches **él**.

The Spanish word for *in* or *on* is **en**. Here's the structure of sentences that express immediate location:

estar + en + the location

> **note:**
>
> **When you talk about where you're from (your place of origin), you use the verb "ser." If you're talking about where you, another person, or an object is at the moment, use "estar."**

2. El loco está en el árbol.

The fool is in the tree.

The fool can hang out for quite some time, but not forever. Since his condition is temporary, we use the verb **estar**.

3. El pollo está en la cocina.

The chicken is in the kitchen.

4. **Estamos en la luna.**

We are on the moon.

In this example, we didn't use a noun or pronoun before **estamos**, because that form of the verb is only used with **nosotros**. **Nosotros** is implied by the verb, so you don't need to say it here.

Using "Estar" to Express Feelings and Emotions

Love comes, love goes...feelings and emotions change with the wind. So use **estar** to talk about them.

Examples

1. ¡Estoy feliz!

I am happy!

2. Estás triste.

You are sad.

3. Ella está loca.

She is crazy.

4. Estamos confundidos.

We are confused.

5. Ellos están borrachos.

They are drunk.

QUIZ III

1) You're in a Latino nightclub. While chatting with a group of Spanish speakers, you detect a mix of accents, which makes you curious. You go around the group asking **"¿De dónde es/son?"** Write in the answer you get from each person or group.

a. María/México:

ella ____ _____ _______________

b. Pedro y Juan/España
ellos ____ ____ ________________

c. Teresa y Susana/Ecuador
nosotras _______ ____ __________________

d. Luis/Uruguay
yo ______ _____ _______________

e. Jose/Colombia
tú ______ ____ _______________________

2) Translate these sentences into Spanish.

a. The chairs are old.
____

b. The trout is stupid.
____

c. We are intelligent children.
____

d. You are crazy Americans.

____

e. She is a slob.

____

3) You're at your friend Susana's party and it's a really rotten fiesta. You call your sister to come pick you up and rescue you from your crummy evening. Your sister wants to know why you're so eager to split. Fill in the gaps in the tale of tragedy that you recount to your sister.

Susana no ______________ feliz. Ella ______________ muy triste. Pedro y Juan ______________ borrachos. Ellos ______________ enfermos. Yo ______________ confundida.

Reminds me of something Shakespeare once said: "Hey, life is pretty stupid, full of hubbub, but not amounting to very much."

- L.A. Story

STRANGE
TALES FROM SPAIN

Jim had always wanted to see a bullfight. He had been fixated on bullfights for each one of his 25 years. Then again, there was a two-month period in 1984 when his world had been nothing but Tempest Bledsoe. But that had passed and the cold comfort of the bulls returned.

The bull fetish had manifested itself in many ways--from waving a red cape at his kid sister to impaling anyone he found wearing sequins. His favorite sport was archery. The only girl he'd dated had been a Taurus. He threw roses at random passersby and feasted on Rocky Mountain Oysters. To blow off steam he liked to hang out at his local China Shop. He had dressed up as a minotaur for Halloween...for seventeen years. When his Uncle Herb had been gored by the horn of a rhino while on safari in Africa, his whole family had wept. Jim was visibly upset.

> **He threw roses** AT RANDOM PASSERSBY, **and feasted on** ROCKY MOUNTAIN **OYSTERS.**

"Dammit!" he thought." Someone this close to me gets gored...Why couldn't it have been by the horn of a BULL!"

Jim certainly was a fan of bulls.

"I certainly am a fan of bulls," he thought. Though, oddly enough, he did not like Michael Jordan.

"I certainly DO HAVE TO PEE A LOT," he would comment TO CO-WORKERS IN THE HALLWAY.

Jim had endured many hardships to come to Spain. He had worked a back-breaking sales job, often working several other jobs at the same time. Eventually, Jim had so many jobs that he didn't have time to actually work any of them. He just went from job to job, sat down, made a face like he was experiencing some pressure in his bladder, then headed for the bathroom; where, in the minds of his co-workers, he would spend the next eight hours.

"I certainly do have to pee a lot," he would comment to co-workers in the hallway.

But peeing was not important now. Now all that mattered was the bulls. He would see a real fight at last. He entered the stadium. It was all he had dreamed of. Screaming fans, a huge bull...and a matador that looked oddly like his Uncle Herb.

"Uncle Herb! You're alive!" shouted Jim.

"That's right!" said Herb, avoiding the charge of a bull. "I faked my own death to pursue my dream of fighting bulls."

Jim was filled with joy. "A relative I once thought was dead is now alive, he's fighting bulls, AND he's offering me a load of bull. Could this be any better?" he thought.

"I love you, Uncle Herb!" yelled Jim.

Distracted by this declaration, Herb let his guard down and the bull drove its horn into his stomach.

It had gotten better. Jim's dream had come true. His uncle had really been gored by a bull.

Jim's mind RACED—what would it be? HIS WHAT? HIS BULL-FIGHTING CAPE?

Jim charged the bull ring surface in a rush of extreme disappointment and orgasmic joy.

He held Herb in his arms as Herb nobly uttered his last words...

"Jim...Jim...you were my nephew...then I was dead...now I am alive and you are my nephew again...I...I...I want you to have..."

Jim's mind raced--what would it be? His what? His bullfighting cape? His matador sword? His custom-made bull-skin comforter?

"I...I...it's very special to me...I...I want you to have my...my Air Jordans."

"NOOOOOOOOOOOOOO!" bellowed Jim, as he gazed into the heavens and longed for the days of Tempest Bledsoe.

Really Basic Stuff

SECTION A: LEARN TO COUNT

Vocabulary

el zoológico - *zoo*
los monos - *monkeys*
las culebras - *snakes*
las plátanos - *bananas*
por favor - *please*
hay - *there is/there are*

In *The Salsa-riffic World of Spanish Part 1*, you learned how to count from 0 to 99. Now we'll teach you to count from one hundred to one million.

When you learned the numbers 1 through 99, you first learned to count from 1 to 29, then you memorized the multiples of ten and tacked on the appropriate single digit number. For example, you learned that to say 76 in Spanish, you add seventy (**setenta**) to the word *and* (**y**), and add on the digit number (**seis**), to get **setenta y seis**.

Just think what you'll be able to do with a few thousand more numbers! You can buy a LOTTERY TICKET FOR A COOL MILLION, play the stock market, count cars on the freeway, and keep track of THE TERMITES IN YOUR WALLS!

The Numbers between 100 and 1,000

The same process applies to the numbers between 100 and 1,000. You just have to memorize the multiples of 100, then tack on the appropriate multiple of ten plus the single-digit number. Here are a few to get you started.

cien **100**

ciento uno **101**

ciento dos **102**

STOP!

Break for a second. Notice that you don't put the "y" after multiples of 100. "Y" only goes between multiples of ten (30 and higher) and single-digit numbers.

ciento treinta y dos **132**

ciento cuarenta y cuatro **144**

ciento noventa y ocho **198**

You probably realized that *100* is **cien**, but *101* is **ciento uno**. That's no mistake, folks--that's how it works in Spanish.

We'll give you the rundown on the difference between **cien** and **ciento**.

- When you want to say 100, you just use the word **cien**.

noventa y ocho	**98**
noventa y nueve	**99**
cien	**100**

"Heh heh, I've got CIEN PLÁTANOS in MY lunchbox!"

- Use **cien** before a noun when you want to talk about 100 of something. For instance, if you want to say you have *100 bananas*, you*The chairs are antiques.* say **cien plátanos**.

- You don't have to worry about gender when you use **cien**, because you can use **cien** with both masculine and feminine nouns. You don't have to change **cien** to make it plural either, since *100* is obviously always plural.

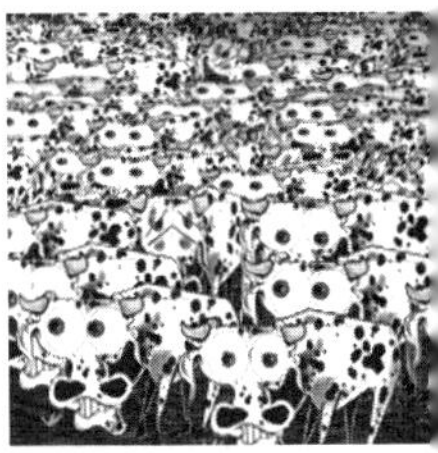

cien vacas

When you're counting numbers between 101 and 199, always use **ciento**. Just tack it onto the numbers 1 through 99, which you've already got down cold.

If you and your friend decide to go cow tipping, and you want to tell your friend how many cows there are in the pasture, you can say:

Hay cien vacas.

There are 100 cows.

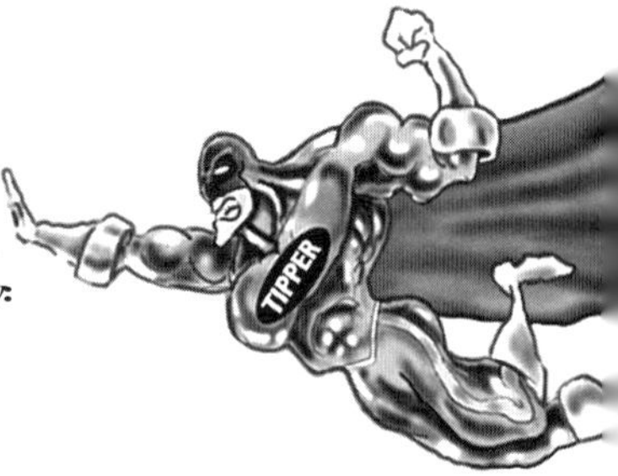

COMPLETE LISTING OF THE NUMBERS BETWEEN 101 AND 120

ciento uno	101
ciento dos	102
ciento tres	103
ciento cuatro	104
ciento cinco	105
ciento seis	106
ciento siete	107
ciento ocho	108
ciento nueve	109
ciento diez	110

ciento once	111
ciento doce	112
ciento trece	113
ciento catorce	114
ciento quince	115
ciento dieciséis	116
ciento diecisiete	117
ciento dieciocho	118
ciento diecinueve	119
ciento veinte	120

You'll notice that small-but-handy word **y** appears again starting with **ciento treinta y uno**. That's because you need to use **y** when you add a single digit to a multiple of ten (larger than thirty, of course)--whether the number is greater or less than 100.

31	**treinta y uno**
131	**ciento treinta y uno**

Multiples of 100

Starting with 200, all the multiples of 100 end in "s." That's because when you have more than one hundred, you're talking about hundreds in the plural.

doscientos	**200**
trescientos	**300**
cuatrocientos	**400**
quincientos	**500**

I never know how much of what I say is true.

- Bette Midler

seiscientos	**600**
setecientos	**700**
ochocientos	**800**
novecientos	**900**

"There's a gender issue with the numbers between 200 and 900."

"When you use these numbers before a noun, the hundreds-place number has to agree in gender with the noun."

"Ah, can't they just agree to disagree?"

"No."

Hay doscientos dieciséis monos y seiscientas cuarenta y dos culebras en el zoológico.

(There are 216 monkeys and 642 snakes in the zoo.)

Let's take that one apart. **Doscientos dieciséis** represents the number *216*. **Monos** means *monkeys* and since it's a masculine noun, we make **doscientos** masculine by ending the word with "os." The "o" makes the word masculine and the "s" is always part of the word **doscientos**.

> **Only the multiples of 100 must match in gender with the noun. None of the other components of the number have to agree in gender.**

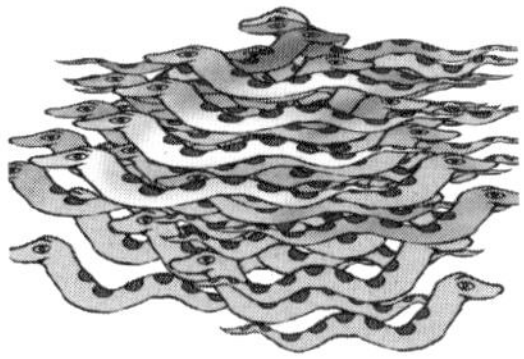

Check out this phrase, campers:

Seiscientas cuarenta y dos culebras.

Culebras, which means *snakes*, is a feminine, plural word. The "a" makes it feminine and the "s" makes it plural. **Seiscientas** has to agree in gender with **culebras**, so it ends in "as." **Cuarenta y dos**, however, does not have to match up.

"Now you can count to 900 with style and grace. On to the thousands!"

Into the Millions

1,000 and Up

The Spanish word for 1,000 is **mil**, and the thousands work like they do in English. Isn't that convenient?

Don't get *mil* confused with the English word million! MIL means ONE THOUSAND.

mil	1,000
dos mil	2,000
tres mil	3,000

Two Important Things about Mil

- When you are talking about more than one thousand, **mil** doesn't become plural like the hundreds-place number does. Instead, the thousands-place numbers translate like in English: *one thousand, two thousand, three thousand,* and so on.

- When you write numbers in the thousands, use a period instead of a comma after the thousands place. That's the way Spanish speakers generally write numbers.

100.000

cien mil *one hundred thousand*

102.000

ciento dos mil *one hundred and two thousand*

With 102,000, you use the form **cien** or **ciento** for 100. It's just like when you were counting between 101 and 199. With numbers in the thousands, you just tack **mil** onto the end to indicate that the number is in the thousands. It's as easy as throwing on a little hot sauce.

cien mil **100.000**

doscientos mil **200.000**

trescientos mil **300.000**

cuatrocientos mil **400.000**

dieciséis millones

cuatrocientos noventa y dos millones, trescientos mil, novecientos cuarenta y cinco

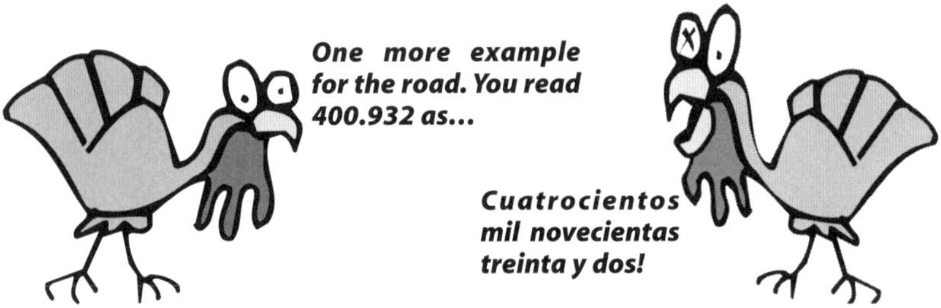

Millions and Millions and Millions and Millions and Millions of Numbers!

The Spanish word for *million* is **millón**. When you get into millions, you have to make **millón** plural the same way you did with hundreds: **millones**. Keep an eye out for accent marks here. The singular **millón** has an accent while the plural **millones** does not.

1.000.000 un millón

2.000.000 dos millones

Try reading these two quick examples out loud to sharpen your counting skills. Turn the book over to check your answers.

16.000.000

492.300.945

SUMMARY

- Use the word **y** (which means *and*) between a multiple of ten and a single-digit number, such as in the number 31 and 131: **treinta y uno** and **ciento treinta y uno**. This applies to numbers larger than thirty.
- When you're talking about numbers greater than 101 and less than 200, use **ciento**.
- Starting with 200, the hundreds place gets an "s" on the end: **doscientos**, **trescientos**, **cuatrocientos** and so forth.
- When a hundreds-place number is paired with a noun, it must match in gender with the noun it modifies.
- Use the word **mil** to indicate thousands, whether you have one or more thousands. **Mil** never becomes plural, nor do you ever have to consider its gender.
- A single *million* is **millón**, which has an accent, but its plural form, **millones**, has no accent

Three o'clock is always too late or too early for anything you want to do.

- Jean-Paul Sartre

SECTION B: TIME TRIPPING

Things like counting, telling time, and talking about seasons and dates are important no matter which language you're speaking or which country you're in. We'll give you some key phrases so you can let someone know that it's hailing outside, or to warn your sleepy roommate that it's the day of her big Spanish exam!

VOCABULARY

el camarero - *waiter*

la camarera - *waitress*

marzo - *March*

septiembre - *September*

¿Qué hora es? - *What time is it?*

THE TIME

Take a look at this short dialog in a Mexican restaurant:

1. **Camarero, por favor, ¿qué hora es?**
Waiter, what time is it, please?

2. **Es la una.**
It's one o'clock.

3. **Gracias.**
Thank you.

Here's the secret to telling time in Spanish: Use the correct form of the verb **ser** plus the hour, just like in the above dialogue.

Put on your 3-D glasses and take a closer look at **es la una**. Obviously the word **una**, which means *one*, is singular --so we use the third-person singular form of the verb **ser**, which is **es**, plus the singular article **la**, since the hours of the day are considered feminine.

As you remember, the verbs **ser** and **estar** mean *to be*. You usually use **ser** to talk about permanent situations or characteristics and **estar** to express locations, situations, or characteristics that are likely to change. We also use **ser** to talk about time. This may seem strange to you on a gut level, since you probably don't think of time as something permanent. You may even feel like running and hiding. But, well, that's just the way it's done in Spanish. Don't worry, pretty soon it'll become automatic and you won't even think twice about it.

The only time you use the singular form **es la** is when you're talking about a time between one o'clock and one thirty. All numbers other than one are plural and therefore take a different form.

¿Qué hora es?

Es la una.

The rest of the time we'll use **son las** to express the time, since we need the plural form. **Las** is the feminine plural article that you need to match the plural number and plural verb.

¿Qué hora es?

Son las once.

Son las cuatro.

Son las seis.

Digressions: The Origin of "o'clock."

Often one person would say to another: "What is the hour?" and the other would reply: "The hour is late." Upon receiving an annoyed look from the questioner, the person answering would often realize, "Oh! Clock!"

What about all those minutes between one full hour and the next? You inquire eagerly. Well, buckaroos, fractions of an hour can be expressed in several ways.

- Use **cuarto**, which means *quarter*.

  Son las once y cuarto.

  It is a quarter after eleven.

- Use **quince**, which means *fifteen*.

  Son las once y quince.

  It is eleven fifteen.

To express the half hour, you also have two options.

- Use **media**, which means *half.*

  Son las once y media.

  It is half past eleven.

- Use **treinta**, which means *thirty.*

  Son las once y treinta.

  It is eleven thirty.

To talk about time between the top of the hour and half past the hour, you just use the hour plus the appropriate number of minutes after the hour. Pretty straightforward.

Son las seis y veintidós.

It is twenty-two minutes after six.

To refer to a time that is after the half-hour, you use the upcoming hour plus the word **menos**, which means *minus,* and then the number of minutes that remain *before* the upcoming hour.

Son las ocho menos diez.

It is ten minutes before eight (or seven-fifty).

Son las dos menos quince.

It is one forty-five.

Es la una y veinticinco.

It is one twenty-five.

Son las dos menos veinticinco.

It is one thirty-five.

Most of our future lies ahead.

- Denny Crum, Louisville basketball coach

The Date

Here's a sentence to chew on.

¿Qué fecha es hoy?

What is today's date?

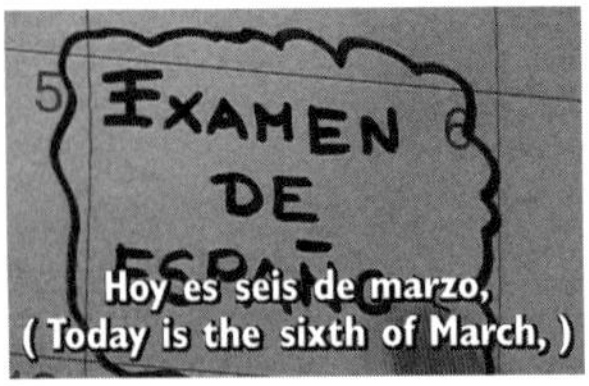

¡HOY ES SEIS DE MARZO,
EL DÍA DE TU EXAMEN DE ESPAÑOL!!!"

Let's break it down, groove masters.

qué	*What*
fecha	*date*
es	*is*
hoy	*today*

NOTE: When you use "qué" as a question word, you must put an accent over the "e."

Ready? Here comes the response to the question, **¿Qué fecha es hoy?**

Hoy es seis de marzo.

Today is the sixth of March.

How does this one work?

- **Seis** actually means *six*, but we translate it as *sixth* in English, since *it's the six of March* would sound weird.

NOTE: You may wonder how to say *sixth* in Spanish. It's **sexto**, but in Spanish you don't use the ordinal numbers (*first, second, third, fourth, etc.*) to indicate the date; you use the cardinal numbers (*one, two, three, four, etc.*)

- The preposition **de** means *of*
- The name of the month, **marzo,** is not capitalized, as you surely remember.

Spanish is a flexible, dynamic language. Just like in English, there is more than one way to ask the date in Spanish. We'll give you a few more appetizing options.

What day is it?

¿A qué fecha estamos?

What day is it?

Hoy es quince de septiembre.

We are on September 15th.

¿Qué día es hoy?

What day is today?

Hoy es quince de septiembre.

Today is September 15th.

¿A cuánto estamos?

What is today's date?

¡Estamos a quince de septiembre!

It's September 15th.

SUMMARY

- To ask the time: **¿Qué hora es?**
- To give the time: A form of **ser** + the hour
- You will always use the plural verb and article **son las** to express time, EXCEPT when you're talking about a time between one o'clock and one-thirty, in which case you use **es la**.
- To express a time after half past the hour: Use the number of minutes it is before the next hour and the word **menos.**
- To ask the date: You have several options, including, **¿Qué fecha es hoy?** and **¿Qué día es hoy?**
- To express the date: Use the article **el** + *number of the day* + **de** + *month*, like in the sentence **hoy es seis de marzo.**

SECTION C: SMALL TALK OR HOW TO TALK ABOUT THE WEATHER

Vocabulary

el tiempo - *weather*

el clima - *climate*

la tormenta - *storm*

el hielo - *ice*

la niebla - *fog*

la niebla gruesa - *thick fog*

el granizo - *hail*

la ropa interior - *underwear*

mucho - *a lot*

malo(a) - *bad*

Notice that **clima** is masculine even though it ends in "a." It's one of those sneaky exceptions to the gender rules.

If you ever find yourself waiting in a doctor's office or in an elevator with a Spanish speaker, you'll need to know how to talk about the weather. Why? Because all humans, regardless of language or place of origin, are genetically programmed to talk about the weather when they have nothing else to talk about. Okay, maybe not, but it's useful to know how to talk about the weather anyway.

When we talk about the weather in English we use the following elements:

it (genderless singular pronoun)

+ *is* (third-person singular form of *to be*)

In Spanish, sometimes we use **estar** to talk about the weather. But with other weather conditions, we use **hace**, the third-person singular form of the verb **hacer**, which means *to make* or *to do*. (Word of Mouth: The easiest way for you to learn these sentences, however, may be to learn them as whole phrases.)

Use **hacer** with the following weather conditions:

Hace frío. - *It's cold.*

Hace calor. - *It's hot.*

Hace viento. - *It's windy.*

Hace sol. - *It's sunny.*

Hace implies *it* or some third-person nonspecific entity, so you don't need a pronoun.

You use **estar** with the following weather conditions:

Está lloviendo. - *It's raining.*

Está granizando. - *It's hailing.*

Está nevando. - *It's snowing.*

Está nublado. - *It's cloudy.*

Notice that **nublado** isn't in the gerund form, although it looks kind of like it.

está + weather condition + gerund

These constructions are easy because they are very similar to English. As with **hace**, you don't have to use a pronoun, because **está** implies a nonspecific, third-person subject. After **está**, you use the weather condition in its gerund form, which is the "i-n-g" form of the verb. For the English verb *raining*, the infinitive form of the verb is *to rain* and the gerund form is *raining*. It works the same way in Spanish. The infinitive is **llover**, and the gerund form (**-ndo**) is **lloviendo**; in the case of *snowing*, **nevar** is the verb and the gerund is **nevando**. The same rule can be applied to **granizar**.

A few thrilling examples of what YOU can say with your new-found vocabulary about weather conditions:

La tormenta es muy mala. Está lloviendo mucho.

The storm is very bad. It's raining a lot.

Está nevando. Hay hielo en las calles.

It is snowing. There is ice on the roads.

La niebla es gruesa.

The fog is thick.

Hace frío. Hay granizo en mi ropa interior.

It is cold. There is hail in my underwear.

SUMMARY

- Use **hace** with the weather conditions *hot* (**calor**), *sunny* (**sol**), *cold* (**frío**), and *windy* (**viento**).

- Use **está** with the weather conditions *rain* (**lloviendo**), *snow* (**nevando**), *hail* (**granizando**), and *cloudiness* (**nublado**).

¡SOY MALO!

QUIZ IV

1) Translate these sentences into Spanish.

a. There are many tables.

____

b. There is a lot of wine here.

____

c. Is there milk?

____

d. There are many restaurants in this town.

____

2) Answer these sentences in Spanish, writing out the numbers.

a. ¿Cuántos meses hay en un año?

____

b. ¿Cuántos días hay en una semana?

____

c. ¿Cuántas estaciones hay en un año?

____

d. ¿Cuántos días hay en un mes?

____

e. ¿Cuántas semanas hay en un año?

____

3) Translate these phrases into Spanish.

a. 100____

b. 100 dogs____________________________________

c. 170____

d. 234 books____________________________________

e. 333____

4) Write these numbers as digits.

a. Doscientos treinta y nueve.

____

b. Noventa y cinco mil cuatrocientos doce.

____

c. Ochocientos cuarenta mil novecientos noventa y nueve.

____

d. Un millón ciento treinta mil quinientos sesenta y dos.

____

e. Ciento catorce.

____

To generalize is to be an idiot.

- William Blake

5) Answer the question, **Qué hora es?** for each of the following.

a. 3:35 ______________________________

b. 5:45 ______________________________

c. 1:30 ______________________________

d. 3:40 ______________________________

e. 9:15 ______________________________

6) Carlos tells you, "Es el nueve de diciembre." What did you ask him? Give at least four possibilities.

a. ______________________________

b. ______________________________

c. ______________________________

d. ______________________________

7) Fill in the blanks.

a. __________ frío.

b. __________ lloviendo.

c. __________ calor.

d. __________ nublado.

e. __________ sol.

f. __________ granizando.

g. __________ viento.

h. __________ nevando.

8) Match the following English phrases with their Spanish equivalents.

a. It is cold.	**1.** Está granizando.
b. It is hot.	**2.** Hace viento.
c. It is sunny.	**3.** Hace frío.
d. It is windy.	**4.** Está lloviendo.
e. It is cloudy.	**5.** Hace calor.
f. It is raining.	**6.** Está nublado.
g. It is snowing.	**7.** Hace sol.
h. It is hailing.	**8.** Está nevando.

9) What is the weather like in each of these seasons? Write a one-sentence description.

a. spring (primavera)

____

b. summer (verano)

____

c. autumn (otoño)

____

d. winter (invierno)

____

10) What time is it? Reply in two different ways.

a. 4:30 ______________________________

____

b. 6:45 ______________________________

____

c. 3:15 ______________________________

____

d. 12:47______________________________

____

e. 1:55 ______________________________

____

SOME GRAMMATICAL STUFF

SECTION A: USING ADJECTIVES

Vocabulary

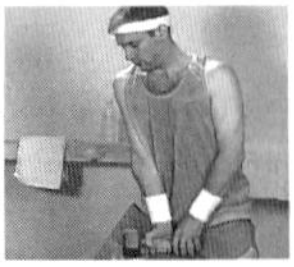

sucio(a) - *dirty*

limpio(a) - *clean*

débil - *weak*

el gato - *cat*

feo(a) - *ugly*

el pájaro - *bird*

la tortuga - *turtle*

alto(a) - *tall*

el conejo - *rabbit*

el ratón - *mouse*

desagradable - *disagreeable*

Rules

We already know that Spanish nouns are considered either masculine or feminine, and that they can be either singular or plural. Adjectives that modify nouns have to match the nouns in gender and number. Also, the placement of adjectives in Spanish sentences is usually different from the placement of adjectives in English sentences.

SUPERSLICK STUDYQUICK
GUIDE TO ADJECTIVES

Adjectives must agree in **gender** and **number** with the nouns they modify.

If an adjective modifies a noun that is **singular** and **feminine**, the adjective must also be **singular** and **feminine**. If an adjective modifies a noun that is **masculine** and **plural**, the adjective must also be **masculine** and **plural**.

Feminine adjectives generally end in **"a,"** and **masculine** adjectives generally end in **"o."** This is usually true of the nouns they modify as well. If you need the adjective to be **plural**, just add an **"s"** to the end of the word.

La historia de Rosa

Rosa, a woman who greatly delights in mud, jumps into a satisfyingly gooey, thick puddle and says with enthusiasm:

¡Estoy sucia!

I am dirty!

Sucio is an adjective that means *dirty*. Since Rosa is a woman talking about herself, she uses the singular feminine form of the adjective. You can tell that **sucia** is singular because it has no "s" on the end.

Manuel, a man who also greatly delights in mud, joins Rosa and frolics with her. Rosa exclaims:

¡Estamos sucios!

We are dirty!

Sucios is the masculine, plural form of the adjective. Rosa uses the masculine form because when you're in a group in which one or more people are male, you use masculine adjectives to describe your group.

Two women approach the mud pit. They look at Rosa and Manuel in digusted amazement. Manuel stops playing for a moment, then points to the women, laughs, and says:

¡Están limpias!

They are clean!

---

limpias - *clean*

- feminine form because it refers to women
- plural form because it refers to more than one woman

FIN.

A few Spanish adjectives end in either "e" or a consonant.

triste - *sad*

débil - *weak*

1. When you use an adjective that ends in "e," such as **triste**, you keep the "e" ending regardless of whether the noun it modifies is masculine or feminine. You only have to consider the noun's number. If your noun is plural, just add "s" to the adjective.

Ella está triste.

She is sad.

The subject (**ella**) is singular and feminine, so we use the singular form of the adjective **triste**. The "e" ending remains just "e." If this woman's melancholy proves contagious and the man gets teary too, we would say:

Ellos están tristes.

They are sad.

Now we have a masculine, plural subject (**ellos**) so we add "s" to the adjective **tristes**. It doesn't matter that **ellos** is masculine. Because

triste ends in an "e," you don't have to consider the gender of the subject, only the number.

2. If you want to use an adjective that ends in a consonant, such as **débil**, use the form **débil** regardless of whether the singular noun is masculine or feminine. If your subject is plural, use the plural form **débiles**. Because **débil** ends in a consonant, you have to add "es" to make it plural--although you might be tempted to, you can't *just* add "s." Sorry, folks.

Ellos son débiles.

They are weak.

In Spanish, the adjective usually goes after the noun it modifies, unlike in English, where the adjective precedes the noun.

el gato feo

the ugly cat

If the cat were a girl cat, you'd say:

la gata fea

the ugly cat

Check out how the adjectives in these book titles agree with the nouns.

El ratón inteligente

The Intelligent Mouse

Los pájaros malos

The Bad Birds

Las vacas rápidas

The Fast Cows

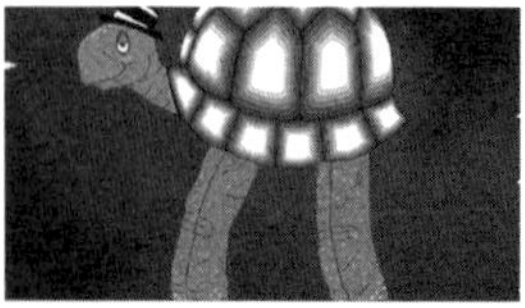

La tortuga alta

The Tall Turtle

Los pollos guapos

The Handsome Chickens

El conejo desagradable

The Disagreeable Rabbit

SECTION B: DEMONSTRATIVE ADJECTIVES

Vocabulary

el toro - *bull*

apestoso(a) - *stinky*

la oveja - *sheep*

estúpido(a) - *stupid*

muy estúpido(a) - *very stupid*

el hombre - *man*

la mujer - *woman*

In English, when we want to point out an object, a place, or a person, we sometimes use words like *this, that, these,* or *those.* When we use these words with a noun, they are called demonstrative adjectives.

Demonstrative Adjectives

Demonstrative adjectives indicate or describe something about a noun the same way regular adjectives do. The reason they're called *demonstrative* is that they demonstrate what or who is being referred to. Spanish demonstrative adjectives, like all Spanish adjectives, must agree in gender and number with the nouns they modify.

This and *these* generally refer to something right in front of you or immediately accessible. Here are the Spanish demonstrative adjectives that mean *this* and *these:*

este	masculine, singular	**estos**	masculine, plural
esta	feminine, singular	**estas**	feminine, plural

Imagine you find yourself in a fragrant field of bulls. If you want to make a statement about a bull right in front of you, you would say:

Este toro es apestoso.

This bull is stinky.

You would use the demonstrative adjective **este** because **toro** is masculine and singular, and **este** is the masculine, singular demonstrative adjective.

The stink continues to rise. You realize that the odor you detect is not emanating solely from one bull, but the entire herd, so you exclaim:

¡Estos toros son apestosos!

These bulls are stinky!

Notice that when you make the sentence plural, every word in the sentence becomes plural.

Having perused the field of bulls to your heart's content, you move on to a field of sheep. After observing a certain sheep for a few moments, you discover that although they are fuzzy and endearing, sheep are not that bright. You declare perceptively:

Esta oveja es muy estúpida.

This sheep is very stupid.

You cleverly use the demonstrative esta because oveja is feminine and singular and esta, being feminine and demonstrative, matches up with it. But you soon realize the limitations of your statement and wish to expand it to include the whole herd. You shout,

¡Estas ovejas son muy estúpidas!

These sheep are very stupid!

Again, all the words in your sentence are in their plural forms to reflect that the subject of your sentence is plural. Of course, you leave the word **muy** alone, because it doesn't have or need a plural form.

NOTE: The demonstrative adjectives **esta** and **estas** look a lot like the second- and third-person singular forms of the verb **estar, está** and **estás.** The crucial difference is that the verb forms have accents over the "a" and the demonstrative adjectives **esta** and **estas** do not.

Since you have mastered the Spanish words **este, esta, estos,** and **estas** with such ease, here's the set of words for *that* and *those. That* and *those* refer to something relatively nearby or accessible, but not necessarily immediately in front of you. It's like when you say *that pile of dirty laundry* as opposed to *this pile of dirty laundry.*

ese	masculine, singular	**esa**	feminine, singular
esos	masculine, plural	**esas**	feminine, plural

Picture this: You and a friend are walking down the street when you see a guy you know stumbling drunkenly along the other side of the street. You nudge your friend in the ribs and say:

Ese hombre está borracho.

That man is drunk.

Ese is the masculine, singular demonstrative adjective for *that*. (Notice we use the verb **estar** as our *to be* verb in this sentence, since drunkenness is generally not a permanent condition.)

Some of the drunk guy's friends show up, staggering and looking goofy. You comment:

Esos hombres están borrachos.

Those men are drunk.

Because there are only men in the group, you use the masculine, plural form of the demonstrative adjective **esos**, as well as the masculine, plural form of the adjective **borrachos**.

One last example. You're in class when you hear the sound of deep, contented snoring. You look up from your notes and see a woman asleep with her eyes open. You chuckle,

Esa mujer está cansada.

That woman is tired.

All the elements in your sentence agree with each other in number and gender. You use **estar** since sleepiness is not usually a permanent condition.

NOTE: The word **mujer** is feminine, even though it does not end in "a." It is one of those exceptions you just need to learn. (Of course, the fact that **mujer** means *woman* should be a big clue.)

Once you have finished formulating your sentence about the sleepy woman, you look around and see that not just one, but several women in the class beginning to nod! You exclaim,

Esas mujeres están cansadas.

Those women are tired.

Let's break down this sentence.

- **Esas** is the demonstrative adjective that means *those*. It is feminine and plural.
- To make **mujer** plural, you just add "es."
- The verb **están**, which is the third-person plural form of **estar**, means *to be*.

Another Demonstrative Adjective

There is a third kind of demonstrative adjective used in Spanish which we don't really have an equivalent for in English. It means *that over there*, implying something or someone farther away or more remote than *this* or *that*.

aquel	masculine, singular	**aquellos**	masculine, plural
aquella	feminine, singular	**aquellas**	feminine, plural

Let's go back to the field of bulls. We already know that one of the bulls is stinky and those other bulls (farther away) are stinky, too. But now, we want to point out that *that bull over there*--even farther away than the others--is stinky, too. You cry out,

¡Aquel toro es apestoso!

That bull over there is stinky!

But that is not enough for you. Oh, no. You must be honest and you must be thorough. Instead of blaming that one poor bull, you correct yourself:

Aquellos toros son apestosos.

Those bulls over there are stinky.

Were you back in the field of sheep, you would feel compelled to make the following observations, in the singular and plural, in reference to sheep a little ways off:

(singular)

Aquella oveja es estúpida.

That sheep over there is stupid.

(plural)

Aquellas ovejas son estúpidas.

Those sheep over there are stupid.

I've always been interested in people, but I've never liked them.

- W. Somerset Maugham

SUMMARY

- Like all Spanish adjectives, demonstrative adjectives must agree in gender and number with the nouns they modify.

- The demonstrative adjectives **este**, **estos**, **esta**, and **estas** generally refer to something right in front of you or immediately accessible.

- **Ese**, **esos**, **esa**, and **esas** generally refer to something relatively nearby or accessible, but not necessarily immediately in front of you.

- The third kind of Spanish demonstrative adjective is one we don't have in English: **aquel**, **aquellos**, **aquella**, and **aquellas**. These mean *that over there*, implying something farther away or even more remote than *this or that.*

QUIZ V

1) Translate these phrases into Spanish. (Check the glossary for hints if you need 'em.)

a. the beautiful horses

____

b. the big mountain

____

c. the new bicycle

____

d. the elegant men

____

e. the good people

____

f. the different tables

____

g. the cute girl

2) Transform these phrases from the singular into the plural or vice versa.

a. el perro blanco

b. los tigres tristes

c. los autobuses amarillos

d. el hombre inteligente

e. el libro nuevo

f. las mesas grandes

____

g. los artículos interesantes

____

h. el viaje agradable

____

i. los profesores serios

____

j. la ciudad mágica

____

3) Change these adjectives to reflect the opposite gender.

a. contento ______________

b. feliz ______________

c. inteligente ________________

d. elegante ________________

e. amable ________________

f. guapa ________________

g. simpático ________________

h. alto ________________

i. tranquila ________________

j. alegre ________________

4) Make these adjectives plural.

a. débil ________________

b. rojo ________________

c. magnífico ____________________

d. loco ____________________

e. estupendo ____________________

f. genial ____________________

g. extravagante ____________________

h. azúl ____________________

i. honrado ____________________

5) In each series, circle the word that doesn't belong.

a. este, esta, ese, estos, estas

b. esos, ese, aquel, esas, esa

c. aquellas, aquel, este, aquella

6) Match each phrase with its English equivalent.

a. aquellas personas	**1.** that book
b. este ejercicio	**2.** these songs
c. estos coches	**3.** this guitar
d. esas mesas	**4.** those moments
e. ese animal	**5.** those cars
f. aquel libro	**6.** those tables
g. aquellos chicos	**7.** this exercise
h. esa guitarra	**8.** those people
i. esos momentos	**9.** those boys
j. estas canciones	**10.** that animal

7) Rewrite the following sentences, changing the words in italics to the singular.

a. Me gustan *estos zapatos.*

____

b. No quiero comprar *estas cucharas.*

____

c. Queremos ir a *esas conferencias.*

____

d. ¿Te gustaría vender *aquellos cuadros*?

____

e. Sería interesante estudiar *esos libros*.

____

8) Fill in the blanks with the appropriate demonstrative adjective: este, esta, estos, estas.

a. ¿Conoces __________ canción?

b. Me gusta mucho _________ pintor.

c. ________ películas antiguas son muy interesantes.

d. ________ actores son muy famosos.

9) Fill in the blanks using the demonstratives: ese, esa, esos, esas.

a. _______ cuento es demasiado largo.

b. ¿De quién son ________ cartas?

c. Me encanta ________ obra de Cervantes.

d. _______ comentarios son de mal gusto.

10) Fill in the blanks using the demonstratives: aquel, aquella, aquellos, aquellas.

a. Necesitamos comprar __________ maleta.

b. Vamos a ________ parque.

c. _______ edificios son los más altos de la ciudad.

d. _______ montañas están muy lejos.

Verb That Word

Verbos (Spanish for *verbs*) are used to describe an action, just like in English. Spanish verbs are organized into three categories:

1. verbs that end in -ar
2. verbs that end in -er
3. verbs that end in -ir

To conjugate a verb, you select the ending you need to match the verb's subject. Regular verbs are conjugated according to a predictable pattern. This is lucky for Spanish students, since once you learn that pattern, you can conjugate any regular Spanish verb.

SECTION A: -AR VERBS IN THE PRESENT TENSE

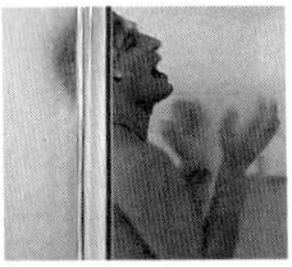

la ducha - *shower*
la lluvia - *rain*
el trabajo - *work*
todo - *everything*

a través de - *through*
la pared - *wall*
el tren - *train*
la lectura - *lecture*

We're just going to tackle present-tense verb endings here. You remember what the present tense is, right? Verbs in the present tense indicate an action happening *right now*. Verb endings match the subject in gender and number, letting you know who is performing the action.

-AR VERB ENDINGS

yo	**-o**
tú	**-as**
él, ella, Ud.	**-a**
nosotros(as)	**-amos**
ellos, ellas, Uds.	**-an**

To use these endings, you drop the -**ar** off the end of the verb and add the ending that matches your subject. Want to see how this works? Bet you do! So here's one for ya: the regular -**ar** verb **cantar**, conjugated in the present tense.

CANTAR (to sing)

yo	**canto**
tú	**cantas**
usted, él, ella	**canta**
nosotros(as)	**cantamos**
ustedes, ellos, ellas	**cantan**

To add a verb ending, drop the **-ar** off the end of the verb and stick the proper ending onto the stem.

c-a-n-t = stem

-a-r = ending that gets dropped

Since the verb ending that goes along with **yo** is **-o**, if you want to say *I sing*, you add the **-o** onto **cant-** and come up with the phrase **yo canto**.

You sing becomes **tú** + **cant-** + **-as**, or **tú cantas.**

Usted, the formal version of the pronoun *you*, uses **-a**, the same ending as a third-person singular pronoun (**él or ella**). So *you* (formal) *sing, he sings,* and *she sings* go like this:

usted **él** **ella**	**canta**

If you want to say *we sing*--whether *we* refers to men or women--you use the ending **-amos** and say either **nosotros** or **nosotras cantamos.**

Ustedes, the plural of *you*, takes the ending **-an**. The same ending is used for **ellos** and **ellas**.

ustedes **ellos** **ellas**	**canta**

> **NOTE:** Keep in mind that pronouns stand for nouns of a particular number and often a particular gender. This is key when you're picking verb endings.

A few sentences in which **cantar** is the **MAIN ATTRACTION**...

Yo canto en la ducha.

I sing in the shower.

Ellos cantan en la lluvia.

They sing in the rain.

¿Usted canta en la clase?

Do you sing in class?

Nosotros cantamos en el trabajo.

We sing at work.

Excelente. Who knew conjugation could be so painless? Let's push the envelope and go through another useful **-ar** verb, **escuchar**, which means **to hear** or **to listen**.

ESCUCHAR (to hear / listen)

yo	**escucho**
tú	**escuchas**
usted, él, ella	**escucha**
nosotros(as)	**escuchamos**
ustedes, ellos, ellas	**escuchan**

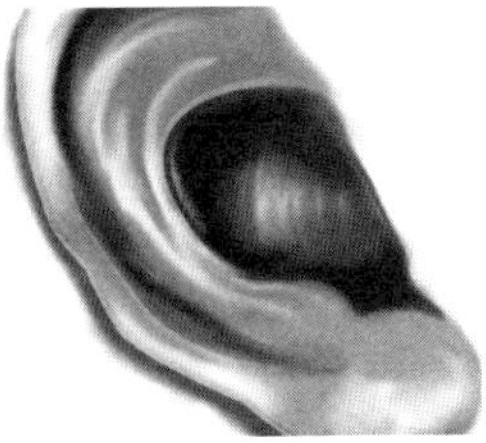

PUTTING THOSE BABIES TO WORK...

Escucho el tren.

I hear the train.

Escuchan el teléfono.

They hear the telephone.

Ella escucha la lectura.

She hears the lecture.

¿Usted escucha a través de la pared?

You're listening through the wall?

SECTION B: -ER VERBS IN THE PRESENT TENSE

Vocabulary

el edificio - *building*

las ardillas - *squirrels*

la nariz - *nose*

los pantalones - *pants*

-er Verb Endings

Present Tense -er Verb Endings		Present Tense -ar Verb Endings	
yo	**-o**	yo	**-o**
tú	**-es**	tú	**-as**
él, ella, Ud.	**-e**	él, ella, Ud.	**-a**
nosotros/as	**-emos**	nosotros/as	**-amos**
ellos/as, Uds.	**-en**	ellos/as, Uds.	**-an**

The only difference between the **-er** verb endings and the **-ar** verb endings is that the "a" is replaced by an "e."

Comer (to eat)

yo	**como**
tú	**comes**
usted, él, ella	**come**
nosotros(as)	**comemos**
ustedes, ellos, ellas	**comen**

EJEMPLOS

Yo como plátanos.

I eat bananas.

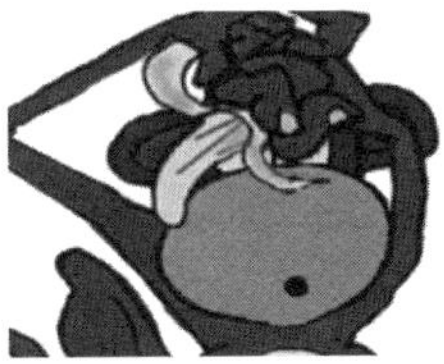

Comemos ardillas.

We eat squirrels.

Él come edificios.

He eats buildings.

Ellos comen pantalones.

They eat pants.

In the first example, the speaker did not need to use the pronoun **yo** since it is implied by the form of the verb **como**.

The ending "o" is only used with **yo**, so it's understood that you mean **yo** when you say **como**. The same is true for the second example, **comemos**, since it can only go with **nosotros**.

BEBER (to drink)

yo	**bebo**
tú	**bebes**
usted, él, ella	**bebe**
nosotros(as)	**bebemos**
ustedes, ellos, ellas	**beben**

A cucumber should be well-sliced, dressed with pepper and vinegar, and then thrown out.

- Samuel Johnson

SECTION C: -IR VERBS IN THE PRESENT TENSE

Vocabulary

el lago - *lake*

grande - *big*

el granero - *barn*

-ir Verb Endings

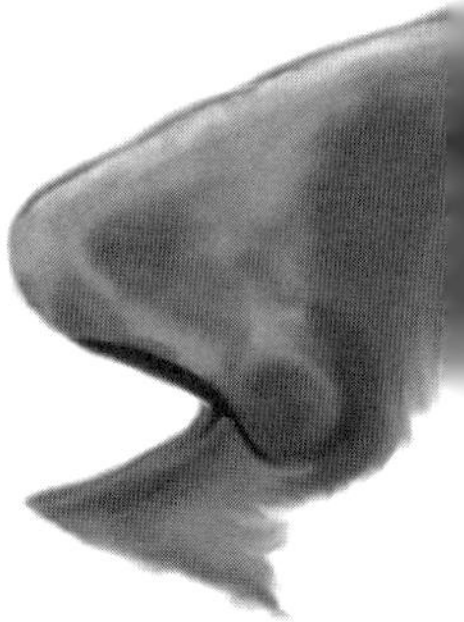

The endings for **-ir** verbs are almost identical to **-er** verb endings...but not exactly. **Bring your nose nice and close to this page** and you'll see that all the endings are the same **EXCEPT** for the **nosotros(as)** ending, which uses an "i."

Present Tense -ir Verb Endings		Present Tense -er Verb Endings	
yo	**-o**	yo	**-o**
tú	**-es**	tú	**-es**
usted, él, ella	**-e**	usted, él, ella	**-e**
nosotros/as	**-imos**	nosotros/as	**-emos**
ustedes, ellos, ellas	**-en**	ustedes, ellos, ellas	**-en**

VIVIR (to live)

yo	**vivo**
tú	**vives**
usted, él, ella	**vive**
nosotros(as)	**vivimos**
ustedes, ellos, ellas	**viven**

Vivo en una ciudad.

I live in a city.

Vivimos en un lago.

We live in a lake.

Viven en un granero.

They live in a barn.

GRUÑIR (to grumble)

yo	**gruño**
tú	**gruñes**
usted, él, ella	**gruñe**
nosotros(as)	**gruñimos**
ustedes, ellos, ellas	**gruñen**

Usted gruñe.

You grumble.

Gruñimos.

We grumble.

SECTION D: THE IRREGULAR VERB "TENER"

VOCABULARY

los jugadores - *players*

el fútbol - *soccer*

los jugadores de fútbol - *soccer players*

el abuelo - *grandfather*

Tener means *to have* in Spanish. Although it's an **-er** verb, it's an **IRREGULAR VERB**. It doesn't follow the predictable regular verb pattern exactly.

Tener Verb Endings

Tener is a stem-changing verb. This means that when you conjugate **tener** you can't just retain the stem **t-e-n** and add the appropriate ending--you have to make an adjustment to the *stem of the verb itself.* Take a look at the conjugation of **tener**.

Tener	**(to have)**	
	yo	**tengo**
	tú	**tienes**
	usted, él, ella	**tiene**
	nosotros(as)	**tenemos**
	ustedes, ellos, ellas	**tienen**

*"Did you get an idea of the changes you have to make when conjugating this verb? You most likely noticed that there is a sneaky "g" in the **yo** form and that an "i" makes its way into all the forms except the **nosotros** form. These oddities make **tener** an irregular verb."*

SUPERSLICK STUDYQUICK

VALUE-ADDED EXAMPLES

Tengo verrugas.

I have warts.

Tú tienes verrugas también.

You have warts, too.

Él tiene verrugas.

He has warts.

Todos tenemos verrugas.

We all have warts.

Time for a little discussion of **USAGE**. You see, Spanish uses the verb **tener** in ways that are different from the way we use *to have* in English.

Basically, tener takes part in several idiomatic phrases that don't translate literally into English. Well, you could translate them literally, but **they'd sound pretty funny**. Just think about English idiomatic phrases like **"it cost an arm and a leg"** or **"I've got a frog in my throat."** No doubt someone learning English as a second language would find these images **amusing**. So just **hang in there** and accept the English translation of such phrases at face value.

1. TENER IS USED TO EXPRESS AGE.

Tengo veinte años.

I am twenty years old.

You may think, "*But that means I have twenty years!*" You're right. Don't bother to translate this idiom literally and it won't rub you the wrong way. Simply tell yourself it means "*I am twenty years old.*"

After you've declared your age, what's the next step? Asking someone else their age, of course!

* English slang for *My stars!*

Things to Notice about This Example:

- This example works when you're addressing someone familiarly--a friend or peer--because it contains the familiar form **tienes**. Do not use this with friendly officers, shopkeepers, or prison wardens, no matter how nicely they may treat you! They would be very insulted.

- **cuántos** means *how many*

- **años** means *years*

- Use two question marks, one upside-down at the beginning of a sentence and one right-side-up at the end, when you phrase a question.

2. TENER DESCRIBES CERTAIN PHYSICAL STATES, SUCH AS HUNGER OR THIRST.

(In English, we would use the verb *to be* in these situations.)

Tengo hambre.

I am hungry.

Tengo sed.

I am thirsty.

Of course, if you are referring to someone other than yourself, you just conjugate **tener** so that the ending agrees properly with the pronoun.

Los jugadores de fútbol tienen sed.

The soccer players are thirsty.

Mi abuelo tiene sed.

My grandfather is thristy.

A SMORGASBOARD OF EXAMPLES TO TITILLATE YOU

1. El tiene frío.
He is cold.

2. Ella tiene alergia.

She has an allergy.

3. Tengo dolor de cabeza.

I have a headache.

4. Usted tiene mucho estrés.

You have a lot of stress.

5. Ellos tienen rosas del jardín.

The have roses from the garden.

Another Irregular Verb: Querer

Querer is another irregular, stem-changing verb which means *to want.* You'll notice similarities between the conjugation of *querer* and *tener,* but stay alert because they're not exactly the same.

QUERER (to want)

yo	**quiero**
tú	**quieres**
usted, él, ella	**quiere**
nosotros(as)	**queremos**
ustedes, ellos, ellas	**quieren**

¡OJO! Notice that when you conjugate **querer**, the stem changes from **q-u-e-r** to **q-u-i-e-r**. Its conjugation is similar to that of **tener**, but be careful: although the first-person, singular form of **tener** is **tengo** with a "g," the first-person, singular form of **querer** is **quiero** -- no "g."

¿Quieres una margarita?

Do you want a margarita?

No. Quiero tres margaritas.

No. I want three margaritas.

¿Ustedes quieren nachos?

Do you want nachos?

No, gracias.

No, thank you.

¿Quieren enchiladas?

Do you want enchiladas?

No, gracias. ¡Queremos salsa!

No, thank you. We want salsa!

IGOR'S SPICY LIME SALSA

3 tomatoes

1 lime

2 jalapeños, fresh

1 clove of garlic

1 Mexican banana pepper

Chop jalapeños and banana pepper. Remove seeds. Mince the clove of garlic and quarter the lime. Dice the tomatoes in a bowl, being careful to save all excess juice.

Mix the jalapeños, peppers, and garlic into the diced tomatoes and juice, stirring vigorously with a fork. Stir and mash more for a liquidy salsa; stir less for chunky salsa.

Squeeze the juice from each quarter of the lime into the salsa mix, then remove the rinds and chop the remaining lime. Add the chopped lime to the salsa and stir again, mixing well.

Add a dash of salt if desired.

I was thrown out of college for cheating on the metaphysics exam; I looked into the soul of the boy next to me.

- Woody Allen

QUIZ VI

1. Fill in the blanks.

a. Yo ________.

b. Tú ________.

c. Él ________.

d. Ud. ________.

e. Nosotros ________.

f. Vosotros ________.

g. Ellos ________.

h. Uds. ________.

2) Write the proper subject pronoun for each of the following phrases.

a.____________ cantamos una canción.

b.____________ bailan flamenco.

c. ____________ tomo una coca cola.

d. ____________ terminas las clases a las dos en punto.

e. ____________ estudia mucho por la noche.

3) Complete the sentences using the present indicative of the following **-ar** verbs. (Use the glossary if you need a hint.)

alquilar **comprar** **cantar** **contar** **gustar**

a. Cada año nosotros ______________ la misma casa.

b. Por las mañanas yo _______________ sellos en el correo.

c. A menudo, él ________________ la misma historia.

d. Mi padre siempre ________________ su canción favorita.

e. Me ________________ tomar mucha agua.

4) Modify the following sentence for each person below.

Leer el periódico.

a. Yo ________________________________.

b. Tú ________________________________.

c. Él/Ella/Ud. __________________________.

d. Nosotros __________________________.

e. Vosotros __________________________.

f. Ellos/Ellas/Uds. ______________________.

5) Write in the correct verb for each sentence, using the present indicative.

vender **comer** **morder** **arder** **encender**

a. Mi padre ________________ la luz para leer el periódico.

b. No _______ pollo. Soy vegetariana.

c. El perro de mi vecino me ____________ cada día.

d. La leña ___________ en la chimenea.

6) You can identify the subject pronouns that correspond to a verb even if you're not sure what the verb means! Try these.

a. almorzamos ____________________

b. coméis ____________________

c. bebe ____________________

d. abren ____________________

e. entreno ____________________

f. participas ____________________

g. cantamos ____________________

h. cenáis ____________________

i. teme ____________________

j. mordemos ____________________

7) Write the infinitive of the following italicized verbs.

a. Nosotros *estudiamos* mucho.

____

b. Ellos *leen* las cartas.

____

c. Vosotros *escribís* con frecuencia.

____

d. Ud. *aprende* español.

____

e. Él *vende* su apartamento este mes.

____

8) Write the subject pronoun that corresponds to each of the following subjects.

a. Pepe y Rosa abren la puerta. ______________

b. Cristina escribe una carta. ______________

c. Mi padres y yo vamos de vacaciones. ______________

d. Tú y tus amigos no creéis en los extraterrestres.

____

d. El profesor habla con sus estudiantes.

____

9) Translate these sentences into Bulgarian. (Okay, fine, you can also translate them into Spanish if you prefer.)

a. I write a book every six months.

____.

b. Peter lives in Spain.

____.

c. She decides a different thing every day.

____.

d. Tina drinks milk every night.

____.

10) Pepe and Juan just met and are now discussing their families. Fill in the blanks in the dialog using forms of **tener**.

a. Pepe: Mi familia es muy numerosa. _______________ tres hermanos y dos hermanas. ¿Y tú, Juan?

b. Juan: Mi familia es pequeña. Sólo _______________ un hermano.

c. Pepe: ¿Sí? ¿Cuántos años _______________ tu hermano?

d. Juan: Mi hermano _______________ quince años. Es más pequeño que yo.

e. Pepe: ¿Cuántos _______________ tú?

f. Juan: _______________ 24 años y...a propósito, me parece que haces demasiadas preguntas.

A Little More Grammar and Some Easy Stuff

SECTION A: JUST SAY NO

Vocabulary

el pescado - *fish (to eat)*

aquí - *here*

Negative Statements

Is there a little black cloud hanging over that woman's head? No, it's not her personal pocket of stormy weather--it's **NEVATIVITY**--something important to know how to express. We'll start off with a basic rule for constructing negative statements in Spanish: Negation words such as *no* or *never* go right before the verb. The word *no* can mean either *no* or *not.*

¡No quiero pescado!

I don't want fish!

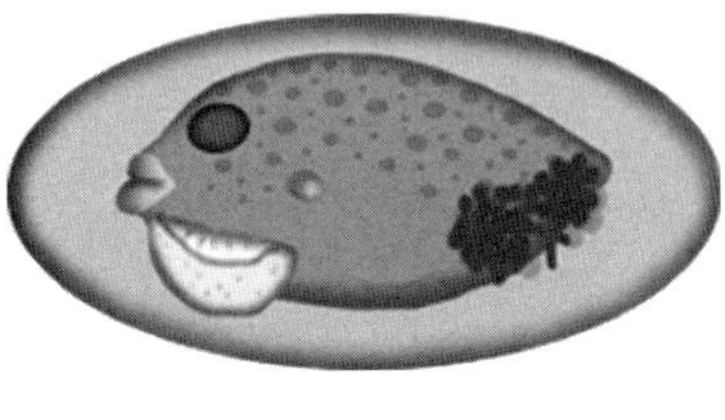

The first word of this sentence is the negation word, *no*. This word lets you know that the speaker is negating the action of the verb.

Not only are double negatives like *not neither* and *not never* permitted in Spanish, they are **positively necessary.**

Él no quiere pescado tampoco.

He doesn't want to fish either.

In the above sentence, the negation word *no* comes right before the verb **quiere**. **Pescado** is the direct object, which follows the verb. Next comes the second negation word: **tampoco**.

If we translated this sentence literally into English, we would say:

He doesn't want fish neither.

"Of course you can't say that in English, but in Spanish it's just ducky."

Other Negation Words for You to Gnaw on:

No hay nadie aquí.

There is no one here.

No tenemos nada.

We don't have anything.

Yo no bebo nunca.

I never drink.

SECTION B: POSSESSIVE ADJECTIVES

Vocabulary

el pulpo - *octupus*

ofensivo(a) - *offensive*

el padre - *father*

los padres - *parents*

el libro - *book*

la motocicleta - *motorcycle*

extraño(a) - *strange*

POSSESSIVE ADJECTIVES
BONUS FAMILY TREE

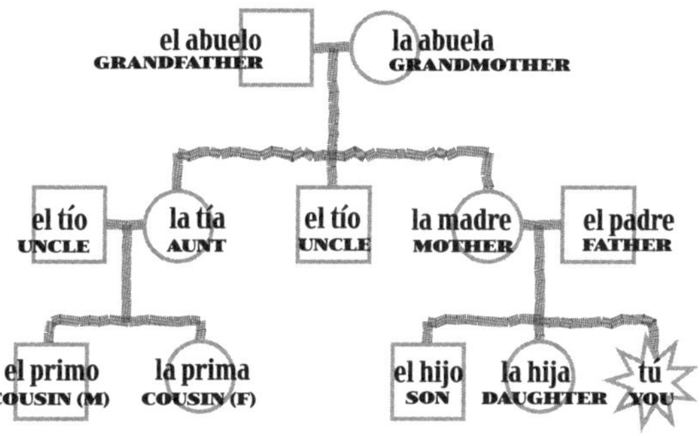

We just learned the verb **tener**, which means *to have*. When you say you have something, you are expressing possession. Another way to express possession in both Spanish and English is by using possessive adjectives.

English	**Spanish (singular)**	**Spanish (plural)**
my	**mi**	**mis**
your	**tu***	**tus**
his/hers/your	**su**	**sus**
*our**	**nuestro/nuestra**	**nuestros/nuestras**

NOTES:

- **Tu** is the informal version of *your*. Notice that **tu** does not have an accent over the "u" like the pronoun **tú** does. This is a case in which an accent distinguishes between two words that are otherwise spelled the same way but have different meanings.
- ***Our*** is the only possessive adjective that reflects gender in addition to number: **nuestro, nuestra, nuestros, nuestras.**

Most adjectives follow the noun in Spanish, but possessive adjectives go before the nouns they modify.

mi perro

my dog

Like all Spanish adjectives, possessive adjectives have to match the nouns they modify.

mi carro

my car

mis carros

my cars

mi roca

my rock

mis rocas

my rocks

tu padre

your father

tus padres

your parents

The possessive adjective **su** and its plural form **sus** go with the formal pronoun **usted.** If you are talking to your professor and referring to her book, you would use the possessive adjective **su.**

su libro

your book

sus libros

your books

Su and **sus** also go with **ustedes**, the plural *you*, as well as with **él**, **ella**, **ellos**, and **ellas**. So **su** can mean *your, his, hers* or *theirs*.

su libro

your book *his book*

her book *their book*

Since **su** has so many meanings, make sure your listener knows who you are talking about!

Possessive adjectives let you know who owns something; but the gender and number of the possessive adjective itself is dependent upon the gender and number of the thing which is possessed.

su motocicleta

his motorcycle

sus calcetines

his socks

If you are talking about *his socks,* you have to say **sus calcetines.** The possessive adjective matches the noun it modifies. In this case, the plural noun *socks* is being modified, so the possessive adjective also must be plural. Just add "s"!

Our has four forms:

1. nuestro **the masculine, singular form**
2. nuestra **the feminine, singular form**
3. nuestros **the masculine, plural form**
4. nuestras **the feminine, plural form**

Nuestra hija es muy extraña.

Our daughter is very strange.

Nuestros hijos son muy extraños.

Our sons are very strange.

The possessive adjectives **nuestra** and **extraña** are singular and feminine, in agreement with the feminine, singularnoun **hija** that it modifies. In the second example, the masculine, plural form, **nuestros**, matches the masculine, plural noun **hijos.** Notice that the adjective **extraños** is in its masculine, plural form in this sentence to match **hijos.**

SUMMARY

- In Spanish, possessive adjectives have to match the noun they modify with regard to number.

- Unlike the other possessive adjectives, **nuestro** expresses gender, so you must make it agree both in number and gender with the pronoun it modifies.

- **Ustedes**, **ellos**, and **ellas** all use the possessive adjective **su** in the singular and **sus** in the plural. With **ustedes**, **su** or **sus** means *your*, and with **ellos** or **ellas** it means *their*.

I met a devil, but he didn't want my soul,

He only wanted to borrow my bike awhile.

- Shel Silverstein

SECTION C: THE SEASONS, THE MONTHS, AND THE DAYS OF THE WEEK

VOCABULARY

el amor - *love*

el aire - *air*

la gente - *people*

la playa - *beach*

las hojas - *leaves*

el ojo - *eye*

THE SEASONS

la primavera

the spring

En la primavera, el amor está en el aire.

In the spring, love is in the air.

el verano

the summer

En el verano, hace sol y hay gente en la playa.

In the summer, it is sunny and there are people on the beach.

el otoño

the autumn

En el otoño, las hojas son bonitas.

In the autumn, the leaves are pretty.

el invierno

the winter

En el invierno, nieva.

In the winter, it snows.

The Months

enero - *January*

febrero - *February*

marzo -*March*

abril - *April*

mayo - *May*

junio - *June*

julio - *July*

agosto - *August*

septiembre - *September*

octubre - *October*

noviembre - *November*

diciembre - *December*

¡OJO! WATCHOUT!
You don't capitalize the months in Spanish.

The Days of the Week

lunes - *Monday*

martes - *Tuesday*

miércoles - *Wednesday*

jueves - *Thursday*

viernes - *Friday*

sábado - *Saturday*

domingo - *Sunday*

¡OJO! WATCHOUT!
You don't capitalize the days of the week in Spanish.

In the Spanish-speaking world, the week starts with **Monday** instead of **Sunday**, which really makes a lot of sense if you think about it.

In English, if we want to indicate something that happens **Monday**, we generally say on **Monday**. In **Spanish**, the article **el** is used, because the days of the week are masculine and singular.

El sábado tengo que estudiar.

On Saturday I have to study.

QUIZ VII

1) Make these sentences negative.

a. Ella bebe mucha cerveza.

____

b. Nosotros vivimos en Andalucía.

____

c. Les gusta esquiar.

_______________________________________.

d. Vosotros jugáis al fútbol.

____.

e. Yo compro todos los caramelos que hay.

____.

2) How else can you make these sentences negative? Check out this example.

Ex: No aprendemos lo que nos enseñan.

Nunca aprendemos lo que nos enseñan.

a. Tú no vienes con nosotros a la fiesta.

____.

b. A María Elena no le gusta viajar.

____.

c. Ellos no participan en clase.

____.

d. La madre no está bien.

____.

3) Fill in the blanks with **nadie** or **nada**.

a. ___________ me ama.

b. A ___________ le gusta perder el dinero.

c. No hay ___________ en el frigorífico.

d. Si ____________ viene, no hacemos una fiesta.

e. Este examen no es ___________ difícil.

4) Answer these questions according to the example.

Ex: ¿Comes siempre a la misma hora?

No, no como nunca a la misma hora.

a. ¿Vas siempre al teatro los fines de semana?

____

b. ¿Cantas siempre cuando estás en la ducha?

____

c. ¿Llevas siempre ese chaleco amarillo?

____

d. ¿Practicas siempre el mismo deporte?

____

5) Give two different English translations for these sentences.

a. No entiendo nada.

____

____

b. No quieres a nadie.

____

____

c. No leen nada.

____

____

d. No me gusta nada.

____

____

6) Fill in the proper possessive adjective and then translate the whole sentence into English.

a. (Ella) ____ árbol.

____

b. (Ellos) _____ zapatos.

____

c. (Yo) ______ padres.

____

d. (Nosotros) ___________ comida.

____

e. (Usted) _________ familia.

____

7) Pepito is asking his friends some questions. Respond to them using the correct possessive adjectives.

a. ¿Es mi casa? __________________________

b. ¿Son tus gafas? __________________________

c. ¿Es su iglesia? __________________________

d. ¿Es nuestra planta?__________________________

e. ¿Es vuestro libro? __________________________

8) Match the following terms.

a. Mis coches	**1.** Our books
b. Vuestros amigos	**2.** His dogs
c. Nuestros libros	**3.** Her letter
d. Su carta	**4.** Your friends
e. Tu lápiz	**5.** My nose
f. Sus perros	**6.** My cars
g. Mi nariz	**7.** Your pencil

9) Translate these sentences into Spanish.

a. I like his car a lot.

____

b. You can come to my house.

____

c. They don't want to listen to our song.

____

10) In each series, circle the word that doesn't belong.

a. primavera, enero, verano, otoño, invierno

b. lunes, martes, febrero, miércoles, jueves

c. enero, febrero, verano, marzo, abril

d. domingo, otoño, lunes, jueves, sábado

STRANGE
TALES FROM SPAIN

It was Christmas morning and Pablo couldn't have been happier. All year long he'd looked forward to this glorious day. For this was the day that all good children were rewarded with gifts: wonderful gifts like sweetmeats and oranges. Pablo bounded down the stairs to the bedroom, barely taking four steps at a time. He'd been a good boy this year and he knew he'd be rewarded. He'd known it ever since the end of May. May. It seemed so long ago, but the memory of that balmy spring morning remained crystal clear. Those boys. The rat. The stones. All the memories came tumbling back as Pablo entered his living room.

It seemed SO LONG AGO, BUT THE memory of that balmy SPRING MORNING REMAINED CRYSTAL CLEAR.

He'd been walking to school when he stumbled upon a small gang of boys throwing stones into the gutter. As he neared the pack of street urchins, he realized that their sticks and stones were hitting the dark gray pelt of a city rat. The rat was bleeding, wounded, and Pablo could see his eyes pleading. The boys cried for Pablo to join in. "Pablo," they cried, "join in!" But he couldn't.

Even though Christmas and its pervasive good cheer was months away, Pablo felt kinship with the rat. Why, in a different place, a different time, he could have been his "rat friend." Pablo jumped in front of the rat. He stared the boys down. He shouted for them to go home. He bravely withstood their taunts... and was stoned within an inch of his life. Nonetheless, he knew that in the stark face of naughtiness, he had been nice. Even then, he could already taste the sweetmeats.

> **Nonetheless,** HE KNEW THAT IN THE **stark face of** NAUGHTINESS, HE HAD BEEN **NICE.**

Pablo sat beneath the Christmas tree. It was the moment of truth. The only time of year to reap the fruits of niceness. He grabbed for a present, tore off the paper, and ripped the lid off the small brown box like a man possessed. There at the bottom of the box was a dead rat. The note inside read,

Dear Pablo,
Some rats are meant to die.

Love,
Santa

P.S. Please enjoy this candy cane.

Pablo smiled and ate the candy cane. It was the best Christmas ever.

OTHER IMPORTANT STUFF

STUFF NO. 1: MORE COGNATES

Although some of these words are written exactly the same way in both languages, others differ in spelling. Here are a few to whet your whistle...

académico - *academic*

el accidente - *accident*

el acelerador - *accelerator*

el activista - *activist*

adicional - *additional*

el apartamento - *apartment*

el barbero - *barber*

la calma - *calm*

el chimpancé - *chimpanzee*

circular - *circulate*

la colección- *collection*

comercial - *commercial*

el comité - *committee*

la democracia - *democracy*

la disciplina - *discipline*

diferente - *different*

la edición - *edition*

la expresión - *expression*

la figura - *figure*

el galón - *gallon*

el garaje - *garage*

la ilusión - *illusion*

importante - *important*

la impresión - *impression*

la literatura - *literature*

la manía - *mania, dislike, craze*

el menú - *menu*

la moderación - *moderation*

nacional - *national*

la ocasión - *occasion*

oficial - *official*

la pasión - *passion*

la planta - *plant*

el problema - *problem*

el programa - *the program*

la reacción - *reaction*

el respecto - *respect*

romántico(a) - *romantic*

el sofá - *sofa*

superlativo(a) - *superlative*

la televisión - *television*

tolerante - *tolerant*

urbano(a) - *urban*

urgente - *urgent*

la versión - *version*

STUFF NO. 2: ACCENTS

Spanish spelling is different from English in that it uses written accents. Stay alert for accent marks and they'll give you an important clue about how to pronounce Spanish words.

In general, you always stress the next-to-last syllable of a Spanish word. However, there are a few exceptions to this rule.

1) Stress the last syllable if the word ends with any consonant except for "n" or "s."

tomar	to take	/toh-MAHR/
moral	moral	/moh-RAHL/
la mitad	middle	/mee-TAHD/

2) Stress the next-to-last syllable if the word ends in a vowel or in the consonant "n" or "s."

el coche	*car*	/KO-chay/
el martes	*Tuesday*	/MAHR-tays/
la copia	*copy*	/KO-pee-yah/

3) The written accent indicates which syllable you should stress.

la religión	*religion*	/ray-lee-hee-ON/
fácil	*easy*	/FA-seel/
el día	*day*	/DEE-yah/

MORE HIGH-PROFILE INFO ABOUT ACCENTS...

Remember to write an accent over any interrogative word you use when you're phrasing a question.

¿qué?	*what?*
¿cómo?	*how?*
¿cuándo?	*when?*
¿dónde?	*where?*

These words also carry an accent when you use them between exclamation marks.

¡Qué sorpresa!

What a surprise!

¡Cómo corres!

How fast you go!

STUFF NO. 3: TRICKY GENDER QUESTIONS

We already established that Spanish nouns, articles, adjectives, and pronouns carry gender, and that most masculine nouns end with an "o" and feminine nouns end in "a." **BUT THAT'S NOT ENOUGH!** Here are some tips for you to deal with any tricky gender questions you might come across.

Nouns ending in **-ción** and **-dad** are feminine.

la silla - *the chair*

la canción - *the song*

la ciudad - *the city*

Some crafty words that end in "a" but are actually masculine.

el día - *the day*

el planeta - *the planet*

el problema - *the problem*

el programa - *the program*

el sistema - *the system*

Some nouns end in something else altogether. You just have to take them on their own terms and learn 'em one at a time.

el lápiz - *the pencil*

el estudiante - *the student*

la leche - *the milk*

el paraguas - *the umbrella*

la naríz - *the nose*

el aceite - *the oil*

la salud - *the health*

STUFF NO. 4: "SER" VS. "ESTAR"

Although both mean *to be,* **ser** usually describes to a permanent condition and **estar** refers to a temporary condition. However, these general rules are not always enough for you to decide which verb to use. This quick reference chart will help you out.

"SER" WORKS FOR...

a) describing people or things

él es estudiante - *he is a student*

b) establishing nationality

soy americana - *I am American*

c) stating origin (use the preposition **de**)

eres de Venezuela - *you are from Venezuela*

d) indicating purpose (use the preposition **para**)

el paraguas es para la lluvia - *the umbrella is for the rain*

e) telling time

son las dos - *it is two o'clock*

f) indicating posession

el coche es de Juan - *the car belongs to Juan*

g) describing permanent personal or physical traits

Teresa es amable - *Teresa is nice*

h) making generalizations

es bueno hacer deporte - *it is good to practice sports*

"ESTAR" WORKS FOR...

a) expressing location

el coche está en el garaje - *the car is in the garage*

b) describing health

Juan está malo - *Juan is sick*

c) expressing a condition at a particular moment

estoy triste - *I am sad*

How to Raise Your I.Q. by Eating Gifted Children

- Book written by Lewis B. Frumkes

STUFF NO. 5: MORE ABOUT "HAY"

Hay is the Spanish equivalent of *there is* or *there are*. Huh? Yes, it does mean both the singular *there is* and the plural *there are*. Take a look at these examples to get an idea of how it works.

(plural)

Hay mucha gente en la calle.

There are many people in the street.

(singular)

Hay algún estudiante americano en esta clase?

Is there an American student in this class?

STUFF NO. 6: NUMBERS AND GENDER

When you're telling somebody how many things you have, always make sure that the numbers and the things they refer to agree in gender.

(plural, masculine)

Tengo doscientos libros en mi casa.

I have two hundred books at home.

(plural, feminine)

Tengo que comprar trescientas cometas para los niños.

I have to buy three hundred kites for the kids.

(with mil)

Hay mil estrellas en el cielo.

There are a thousand stars in the sky.

(with millón)

Conozco un millón de personas.

I know a million people.

(with millones)

¡Ojalá que tuviera tres millones de pesetas en el banco!

I wish I had three million pesetas in the bank!

STUFF NO. 7: HICKORY, DICKORY, DOCK

As in English, there is more than one way to ask for the time in Spanish. The most common way is to say, **¿Qué hora es?**, but you can also ask, **¿Tiene Ud. la hora?**

QUÉ HORA ES?

Son las dos y cuarto.

It's a quarter after two.

Son las dos y media.

It's half-past two.

Son las dos menos cuarto.

It's a quarter to two.

You can also just read the numbers off the clock, like in English.

Son las tres y cuarenta y cinco minutos.

It's three forty-five.

Son las ocho y veinticinco.

It's eight twenty-five.

STUFF NO. 8: DATES

When you want to ask what day it is, you have a number of options. All of these are equally correct and appropriate.

¿Qué fecha es hoy?

¿A qué fecha estamos?

¿A cuánto estamos hoy?

¿Qué día es hoy?

Reply to each of these questions by using the same verb and format that appeared in the question.

¿Qué fecha es hoy?/ ¿Qué día es hoy?

Hoy es trece de mayo.

Today is May thirteenth.

¿A qué fecha estamos?/ ¿A cuánto estamos hoy?

Hoy estamos a trece de mayo.

Today is May thirteenth.

¿Qué fecha es hoy?	**Hoy es diecisiete de junio.**
What's today's date?	*Today is June 16th.*

¿A qué fecha estamos?	**Estamos a quince de enero.**
What's today's date?	*Today is January 15th.*

STUFF NO. 9: WHAT THE HECK IS NOUN-ADJECTIVE AGREEMENT?

It's not as complicated as it sounds. In fact, you probably have a good handle on noun-adjective agreement after watching *The Salsa-riffic World of Spanish Part 1 & 2* and studying this *Study Sidekick*. In Spanish, adjectives must agree in gender with the nouns that they modify. If the noun is feminine, then the adjective must also be feminine. If the noun is masculine, then the adjective must also be masculine. You get the idea.

una silla blanca

a white chair

un gato negro

a black cat

Moreover, adjectives must also always agree with the noun in terms of number. If the noun is plural, then our adjective must also end with an "s."

Los libros baratos.

Cheap books.

Las casas bonitas.

Pretty houses.

Whenever an adjective ends in "e," we don't have to consider the gender of the noun it modifies, we only have to figure out whether or not the noun is plural in number.

Los niños tristes.

The sad boys.

Las clases interesantes.

The interesting classes.

Azúl becomes **azules** in its plural form.

...and *blue* stays *blue.*

In Spanish, descriptive adjectives like these almost always follow the noun they modify.

El coche rojo.

The red car.

La mesa bonita.

The pretty table.

STUFF NO. 10: DEMONSTRATIVE ADJECTIVES

Like descriptive adjectives, demonstrative adjectives must also agree in number and gender with the noun they modify. There are three types of demonstratives:

a) Demonstrative adjectives that refer to something close to the speaker.

este or **esta**, which mean *this*

estos or **estas**, which mean *these*

Me gusta esta mesa.

I like this table.

No entiendo estos ejercicios.

I don't understand these exercises.

b) Demonstrative adjectives that refer to something farther away, yet still accessible to the speaker.

ese or **esa**, which mean *that*

esos or **esas**, which mean *those*

¡Qué bonito es ese perro!

What a pretty dog that is!

Esos libros son interesantes.

Those books are interesting.

c) Demonstrative adjectives that refer to something even farther away from the speaker.

aquel or **aquella**, which mean *that over there*

aquellos or **aquellas**, which mean *those over there.*

I like a woman with a head on her shoulders. I hate necks.

- Steve Martin

Aquella casa está lejos.

That house is far away.

Aquellos coches son grandes.

Those cars over there are big.

STUFF NO. 11: THE PRESENT INDICATIVE REVISITED

When we're conjugating a verb in the present indicative, the first thing we must do is take a look at the verb's ending. Does it end in **-ar**, **-er**, or **-ir**? Once we have figured out what kind of verb it is, there's only one thing left to do.

Drop the -ar, -er, or -ir ending and replace it with the correct new ending!

As we have seen, each type of verb has its own set of endings. Here's a handy chart.

TYPE OF VERB: **-ar** verbs like **cantar, almorzar, amar,** and **hablar**

ENDINGS: **-o** (**yo**), **-as** (**tú**), **-a** (**Ud., ella,** or **él**), **-amos** (**nosotros**), **-áis** (**vosotros**), **-an** (**Uds., ellas,** or **ellos**)

TYPE OF VERB: **-er** verbs like **vender, comer, beber,** and **saber**

ENDINGS: **-o** (**yo**), **-es** (**tú**), **-e** (**Ud., ella,** or **él**), **-emos** (**nosotros**), **-éis** (**vosotros**), **-en** (**Uds., ellas,** or **ellos**)

TYPE OF VERB: **-ir** verbs like **vivir, partir, abrir,** and **dormir**

ENDINGS: **-o** (**yo**), **-es** (**tú**), **-e** (**Ud., ella,** or **él**), **-imos** (**nosotros**), **-ís** (**vosotros**), **-en** (**Uds., ellas,** or **ellos**)

STUFF NO. 12: NO. NOTHING. NO ONE. NEVER!

We can always make a sentence negative by simply adding the word **no** before the verb.

No como carne. - *I don't eat meat.*

¿No te gusta la cerveza? - *Don't you like beer?*

The word **nunca** (*never*) is also placed before the verb.

Nunca voy al cine. - *I never go to the movies.*

Ellos nunca dicen la verdad.
They never tell the truth.

Another way to use nunca is to create a sentence with a double negative.

El no lee nunca. - *He doesn't ever read.*

¡OYE¡ HEY!

This is perfectly legal in Spanish. It's not like taking the tags off your pillows or anything.

The double negative in the previous example emphasizes the negativity expressed in the sentence. While in English we say, *I don't like anybody/anything* or *I like nobody/nothing*, in Spanish we have to say, **No me gusta nadie/nada.**

> **Ella no quiere pescado tampoco.**
>
> *She doesn't want fish either.*

What about the negative words **nadie** (*nobody*) and **nada** (*nothing*)? All right, fine, we'll give you a few examples.

> **Nadie está interesado en esa lectura.**
>
> *Nobody is interested in that reading.*

> **Nada me puede hacer cambiar de opinión.**
>
> *Nothing can make me change my mind.*

There you go...and that's all the Other Important Stuff you need to know!

ARRIBA, ARRIBA!

STRANGE
TALES FROM SPAIN

It was afternoon in the royal palace and things were slow. That happened a lot when you were part of a vestigial monarchy. The king used to be involved in the day-to-day ruling of the country, but now his role consisted mostly of making public appearances at international balls and the grand openings of municipal swimming pools. So the king wasn't all that upset when the crazy-looking man wearing a beret and a tunic burst into his office.

Marco Suarez had always prided himself on being a visionary. Where others saw a vacant lot, he saw a four-star hotel. Where some saw a junker, he saw a refurbished classic. On the other hand, where some saw corners, he saw little demon men drinking the blood of babies. But hey, sometimes there's a worm in your melon, right?

> ON THE OTHER HAND, **where some** saw corners, he saw LITTLE DEMON MEN DRINKING **THE BLOOD OF BABIES.**

"I am a visionary," he announced, standing before the king. "And I have found a new frontier. We must sail west. That way we will find a quicker route to the Spice Islands and our empire will become mighty through spice."

The king's on-the-spot-decision-making experience consisted of deciding whether or not to put on pants in the morning. He responded accordingly.

"Aaaaahhh..."

"I have come to you for funding," explained the visionary. "I will use the money to purchase three ships. I will sail west, heading for the Spice Islands. Instead I will stumble upon a new, undiscovered world, which we will eventually lose to the English, who will eventually lose it to the Americans, who will go on to name a holiday after me which will enable working men and women to have an extra day off, allowing them more time to go to the dump and to do yard work, but not go to retail stores, for they will be closed in observance of this great day."

...HE BEGAN THROWING **things at the corners** OF THE ROOM AND SCREAMING "SOMEONE MUST SAVE THE **BABIES!"**

"I...I think that already happened," said the king, remembering a calendar he had looked at once while trying to decide whether or not to put on pants.

But since he wasn't sure, and since he was the king and he did sleep on a mattress stuffed with pesetas, he decided to give Marco some money anyway--because he had provided the king with some excitement and because he began throwing things at the corners of the room and screaming "SOMEONE MUST SAVE THE BABIES!"

Marco took the money and sailed west. When he got there, he discovered a land. Sure enough, the king was right. Someone had discovered it before him. If he wanted to have a day in his honor, he would have to be a visionary in some other way. So Marco decided to run for president--and he did. And once in office, he had himself assassinated. So now, thanks to Marco, September 23rd is a day off...for crazy people.

MUCHAS GRACIAS, MARCO.

PRACTICE EXAM I

1) Underline the diphthong in each word.

a. idiota

b. buena

c. magia

2) Write a word that contains the letter *ñ*.

____

3) Translate the title of this book into Spanish. (Rememner to capitalize the Spanish way!)

Beloved Intelligent Boy

____

4) Translate this phrase into Spanish, capitalizing where necessary.

President Aznar__________ __________

5) Write out these phone numbers in Spanish.

a. 3-25-33-78

b. 7-44-56-98

c. 4-23-61-70

d. 6-88-06-16

e. 1-94-22-51

6) Roberto and Margarita run into each other on campus. Please fill in the blanks of the following dialog between them:

a. Margarita: __________ __________, Roberto.

b. Roberto: Buenos días, Margarita. ¿__________ __________?

c. Margarita: Muy bien, gracias. ¿ ________ ________?

Roberto: Así, Así.

d. Margarita: ¿_____ __________ __________?

e. Roberto: A mi clase de historia. ¿_____ ________?

Margarita: A mi clase de historia también.

Roberto: Bueno, tengo prisa. ¡Hasta luego!

f. Margarita: ¡______________!

7) Write the definite article for each of these Spanish words.

a. __ guitarras

b. __ naranjas

c. __ niños

d. __ teteras

e. __ zapato

8) Write the plural for each of these articles and nouns.

a. el queso ___ ______________

b. un aguacate ___ ______________

c. el piano ___ ______________

d. la rosa ___ ______________

e. los tostadores ___ ______________

9) You are in your favorite cheese shop when a few Latin Americans show up. Feeling friendly toward your fellow cheese-lovers. you strike up a conversation, asking in your best Spanish, "**De dónde es/son?**"

a. Rosa/Guatemala

usted _____ _____ ______________

b. Carmen y Florencia/Honduras

vosotras ____ _____ ______________

c. Fernando y Pedro/Venezuela

ustedes _____ _____ ______________

d. Ana y Adriana/Costa Rica

ellas _____ _____ ______________

e. Ricardo/Agentina

el _____ _____ ______________

10) Translate these sentences into Spanish.

a. I am a dentist.

____

b. The cookies are free.

____

c. The train is fast.

____

d. The shoes are yellow.

____

e. We are young and beautiful.

____

11) Translate these sentences into Spanish.

a. She is in the hospital.

____

b. Juan and Pedro are in the cafeteria.

____

c. We are in Spanish class.

____

d. They are in the bakery.

____

e. I am in bed.

____

12) Fill in the blanks with either **ser** or **estar**.

a. Pedro y Juan _____ hoy en Nueva York.
b. Ricardo _____ de Florida.
c. La trucha _____ estúpida.
d. Los americanos ______ locos.
e. Nosotros ________ contentos.

PRACTICE EXAM 2

1) Translate these sentences.

a. There isn't any water.

____

b. There are too many people here.

____

c. There aren't many cars.

____

2) Answer the questions.

a. ¿Cuántas horas hay en un día?

____

b. ¿Cuántos segundos hay en un minuto?

____

c. ¿Cuántos minutos hay en una hora?

____

d. ¿Cuántos minutos hay en un cuarto de hora?

____

e. ¿Cuántos segundos hay en dos horas?

____

3) Write out these numbers in Spanish.

a. 458

____

b. 1,000

____

c. 2,600

____

d. 1,000,000

____

e. 2,500,000

____

4) Write these numbers in digits.

a. novecientos noventa y nueve mil novecientos noventa y nueve

____

b. trescientos treinta y cinco

____

c. quinientos cincuenta y seis

____

d. ocho millones cuatrocientos mil ochocientos ochenta y ocho

____

e. doscientos treinta y dos mil trescientos veintidos

____

5) Write out the time in Spanish.

a. 4:15 ______________________________

b. 6:00 ______________________________

c. 1:45 ______________________________

d. 11:30______________________________

e. 12:00______________________________

6) Give two different ways of answering "**¿Qué hora es?**"

a. 8:35

____

____

b. 9:30

____

____

c. 11:40

____

____

d. 7:50

____

____

e. 1:15

____

____

7) Fill in the blanks with the appropriate month of the year.

a. Hace frío en ________________.

b. Hace sol en ________________.

c. Hace calor en ________________.

d. Está granizando en ________________.

e. Está nevando en ________________.

f. Hace viento en ________________.

8) What's the weather like in the following places?

a. California

____

b. Seattle

____

c. Chicago

____

d. Alaska

____

e. Texas

____

9) Fill in the blanks.

a. Las tortugas felic___.

b. Los barcos bonit___.

c. Los restaurantes car____.

d. Las canciones hermos____.

e. La gente agradab____.

10) Change these phrases from the singular to the plural or vice versa.

a. El limón amargo.

____

b. La habitación grande.

____

c. El niño listo.

____

d. El pueblo blanco.

____

e. El poeta bueno.

____

f. Las chaquetas verdes.

____

g. Las manos finas.

____

h. Las orejas gordas.

____

i. Los pies olorosos.

____

j. La pared pintada.

____

11) Change these adjectives to reflect the opposite gender.

a. actual ______________________

b. magnífico ______________________

c. extravagante ______________________

d. loca ______________________

e. rápido ______________________

12) Rewrite the following sentences, making the italicized words singular.

a. Aquellas casas son muy modernas.

____

b. ¿Te apetecería comer estos pasteles?

____

c. No me gustan esos juegos de mesa.

____

d. Contesta estas preguntas por favor.

____

e. Aquellas chicas son españolas.

____

13) Fill in the blanks with the appropriate demonstrative adjective: **este, esta, estos, estas.**

a. ¡Qué hermosos son ________ caballos!

b. ________ playa es muy limpia.

c. Mañana voy a ________ bar.

14) Use **ese, esa, esos, esas** in the following sentences.

a. __________ examen es muy fácil.

b. ¿Cuánto cuesta ___________ camisa azúl?

c. Yo cocino ______________ comidas en mi casa.

d. ___________ hombres son buenos.

15) Fill in the blanks using the demonstratives: **aquel, aquella, aquellos, aquellas.**

a. _____________ museo es muy interesante.

b. La oficina de turismo está en ____________ calle.

c. ____________ turistas llevan cámaras de fotos.

d. Yo conozco a ________________ chicas americanas.

16) Answer the following questions in the present indicative tense.

a. Yo __________ (hablar) en español e inglés.

b. Ellos __________ (saber) bailar el flamenco.

c. Cuando están en casa, ellos siempre __________ (comer) algo.

d. Para mi cumpleaños mi madre me __________ (preparar) un pastel.

e. Muchas veces tú __________ (escribir) demasiado rápido.

17) Translate the following into Spanish.

a. They eat every day at five o'clock.

____

b. I drink a lot of water.

____

c. You (pl.) talk four different languages.

____

d. My mother writes her recipes in her book.

____

18) Give the infinitive of the following italicized verbs.

a. No *entiendo* muy bien la pregunta.

____

b. El profesor *explica* la lección.

____

c. *Queremos* ir a la fiesta.

____

d. Ellos se *marchan* hoy.

____

e. Vosotros *tenéis* muchos coches.

____

19) Lola and Carlos are conversing at the university. Please fill in the blanks.

Lola: Qué día tan bonito. No __________ (querer) irme a casa tan temprano. ¿Nos __________ (tomar) algo en un bar.

Carlos: Me encantaría. Me __________ (gustar) estar en la calle. ¿Te __________ (gustar) ese bar?

Lola: Sí. Hay buenas tapas allí. Vámonos.

20) Translate these sentences into Spanish.

a. Peter wants to drive a car.

____

b. María and Felipe want to sing a song.

____

c. Nosotros want to learn Spanish.

____

d. They want to travel to Spain.

____

21) Answer the following questions according to the example.

Ex: **¿Comes siempre en la universidad?**

No, no como nunca en la universidad.

a. ¿Bebes siempre coca cola?

____

b. ¿Usas siempre gafas para leer?

____

c. ¿Te gusta siempre estar con tus amigos?

____

> Give me ambiguity or give me something else.
>
> - Bumper sticker

d. ¿Lees siempre un libro en la cama?

____

e. ¿Vas siempre al cine a ver una película?

____

22) Fill in the proper possessive adjective and translate the whole phrase into English.

a. (él) ________ clases. ______________________

b. (vosotros) ________ trabajos. ______________________

c. (tú) ________ coches. ______________________

d. (ustedes) ________ dinero. ______________________

23) For the following sentences, replace the underlined definite article with the correct possessive adjectives.

a. Lleva monedas en <u>el</u> bolsillo. (usted)

____

b. Llamo a <u>la</u> casa para hablar con ella. (yo)

____

c. Escribís las recetas en un papel. (vosotros)

____

d. Hablas con la profesora después de clases. (tú)

____

e. A las siete, se van en el avión privado. (ellas)

____

24) Match the following terms.

a. enero	**1.** Monday
b. invierno	**2.** autumn
c. lunes	**3.** Friday
d. primavera	**4.** May
e. verano	**5.** winter
f. viernes	**6.** Sunday
g. domingo	**7.** January
h. otoño	**8.** September
i. mayo	**9.** spring
j. septiembre	**10.** summer

STRANGE
TALES FROM SPAIN

Roberto was the finest amateur boxer in his village. He'd had his first fight when he was only eight years old. It was in the school yard of the Montalban Elementary School, with a younger boy named Pedro. He'd asked Pedro for his lunch money. Pedro refused. Roberto apologized, shook his hand, and punched him in the back of his head when he turned to leave. As Pedro hit the cement floor of the school yard, a prizefighter had been born in Roberto.

Roberto's amateur career was rocky at first. His manager loved Roberto like a son and was often overprotective. For the first eight months, he allowed Roberto to fight only cowardly weaklings and eighty-year-old men. After his first week of fighting, his record was an astonishing 59 and O. But Roberto soon grew tired of his one-round, slaughterhouse victories. One day, after a quick victory over "Flaccid Joe," Roberto approached his manager.

ROBERTO APOLOGIZED, **shook his hand,** AND PUNCHED HIM IN the back of his head when HE TURNED TO LEAVE.

"Miguel," he said, "I want to fight a winner. A man in his prime."

"But Roberto," Miguel answered, his voice shaky and unsure, "I've just lined up a bout with 'Sugar Ray Crotch-Kicker'!"

Roberto stood firm. "No, Miguel. It's time to be a champion. It's time to fight."

Roberto acquiesced and arranged a professional bout with "Iron Fists Castilla," an undefeated fighter. The fight would take place in three weeks. Roberto trained like never before. He ran and sparred. He sparred and ran. In no time at all, it was the night before the fight, and Roberto Consuela was in the shape of his life.

The consummate sportsman, Roberto went to Iron Fist's house to wish him luck. But when he knocked on his door and Castilla opened it he was struck by an unexplainable wave of intense pride.

"Castilla," he said with a smirk, "you will drop in one."

CASTILLA SMILED BACK and without A WORD HE SHATTERED ROBERTO'S RIBS.

Castilla smiled back and without a word he shattered Roberto's ribs. For the next five minutes Roberto flopped around like a rag doll as Iron Fists hit him with a barrage of hurricane-speed punches. Then, in a flash, Castilla slammed the door. Roberto gasped on the ground. He was beaten.

Roberto limped home, his head hanging low. He'd thought he was a champion. Sadly, he now knew that Castilla would destroy him. He would lose the fight and the rest of his pride.

That night, Roberto barely slept. But as the hours wore on, Roberto's confidence began to creep back. He was Roberto Consuela, his father's son, and he didn't have to lose this fight.

And so Roberto Consuela did what only a man could do. That night, he crept into Iron Fist's house and hit him in the face with a board.

THE ANSWER MAN

The Answer Man is dedicated to alleviating the worries of his fellow Cerebellum employees. Each day, he receives hundreds of letters from co-workers. We have reprinted some of them here with The Answer Man's responses. We hope they can be helpful to you, too.

Dear Answer Man,

1. What is the Middle East in the middle of?
2. Who are you before you are born?
3. Why / When did they switch from straight screws to Philip's head screws?
4. Who is Phillips?
5. Was cottage cheese originally made in a cottage?

Please help, can't sleep with these burning questions on the loose.

> **1. The Middle East is in the middle of a very difficult stage in its development. Don't give it a hard time.**
>
> **2. An avatar of Charlton Heston.**
>
> **3. They did in 1982, when the Phillips Company bought the Standard Head Company.**
>
> **4. Phillips is the owner of Phillips Company. He is 34, unmarried, and enjoys raising pookahs and lop-ears.**
>
> **5. Yes.**

Dear Answer Man,

Yesterday I was speaking with my cat, Annie, and she believes the best way to woo the opposite sex is with dinner and a moonlight stroll. But I am of the opinion that this is a cliched dating ritual. Wouldn't one impress the opposite sex more if she or he did something more unique and personal on a date? Please help solve our debate.

Hmm. I would counter that what works on a date is a very personal thing. Like a good salesperson, you have to gauge your datee and decide what he or she will respond most favorably to. Then, you have to jump in for the kill. So while I would say that Annie has good instincts, she needs more experience. But she is four, and you know how cats get when they're four, they think they know everything.

DO YOU

have a question for the Answer Man?

Send your questions about life, love, and the world in general to:

THE ANSWER MAN
2890 Emma Lee Street
Falls Church, VA 22042

Dear Answer Man,

Why does my mom eat cheese?

Whipped cream and milkshakes aren't enough.

Dear Answer Man,

Is there anything you think I should know?

Um...no.

CRUCIGRAMA ESPAÑOLA

ACROSS

3 Freebee
5 Tuxedo-wearing cold-weather bird
8 Caffeine injection
10 Often pulled out of a hat
11 A -- is a -- is a --
12 Hunka hunka burnin' love
14 Comes in red, white, and rose
15 Bye-ya
17 Pretty -- with sugar on top
20 First day of the week
23 Month when witches ride
25 Add to your cafe
27 Too much cerveza
28 Eat this when you're monkeying around
29 Good morning
30 What's up?

DOWN

1 A stinky bull
2 Jersey-wearing ball-kicker
4 From the U.S.A.
6 Fill in your --, address, and phone number
7 He's always got his -- in my business
9 Honorable occupation of scribe
13 Opposite of "with it"
16 Don you --- and let's ride!
18 Moo
19 Girl with a messy room
21 Delicious veggie treat
22 Por autobus, avion, o --
24 Kind of fish
26 Impolite expulsion

¡Qué rico! Word Search

P	I	C	A	N	T	E	C	R	O	A	E	S	B	E
C	G	A	T	O	L	A	E	R	T	D	O	O	U	D
A	A	N	G	O	I	D	A	S	I	T	M	C	E	N
F	R	A	R	U	R	J	I	F	N	A	S	O	N	A
E	B	Z	E	A	A	T	I	E	R	V	A	C	A	R
R	E	N	S	P	R	C	I	G	A	S	C	P	S	G
B	L	A	T	A	I	S	A	L	E	L	I	E	N	N
M	U	M	A	O	O	R	E	T	L	U	H	S	O	S
O	C	R	U	L	I	N	N	I	E	A	C	C	C	O
H	I	S	R	T	T	A	L	E	U	B	A	A	H	R
A	U	O	A	I	U	E	E	N	C	E	N	D	E	R
J	D	I	N	G	T	L	D	I	N	E	R	C	S	U
E	A	D	T	N	E	O	L	L	A	B	A	O	S	C
V	D	A	E	M	P	A	N	A	D	A	L	T	O	H
O	O	G	C	U	N	P	L	E	A	N	O	S	O	D

Look through the scrambled letters for each of the words listed below. Circle each letter of each word as you find it. When you circle all of the letters of all of the words, there will be some letters left over. Make a list of the unused letters and the unscramble them to solve the puzzle. (Solution: 9 letters)

ABUELA	ADIOS	AGUACATE	ALTO
ARDER	ARTISTA	BAUL	CAFE
BUENAS NOCHES	BURRITO	CABALLO	COCOS
CHICAS	CHURROS	CIUDAD	EDIFICIO
CULEBRA	CUMPLEANOS	DINERO	GENTE
EMPANADA	ENCENDER	GATO	LO SIENTO
GRANDE	GUANTES	HOMBRE	OVEJA
MANZANA	MARGARITA	NOCA	REAL
PAJARO	PESCADO	PICANTE	
RESTAURANTE	TORTILLA	VALENTINE	

Flan de la Mamita de Rachel

- 11 heaping teaspoons of white sugar
- 4 eggs (one per person)
- 3 cups milk
- 1 teaspoon vanilla
- 4 t. cinnamon

Preheat oven to 400 degrees. Using oven mitts or something else to protect your tender flesh, heat a ring-mold baking pan over a very low heat. After the baking pan has heated up, pour seven heaping teaspoons of sugar into the pan. The sugar will melt and turn into dark brown caramel. As the sugar is melting, tilt the pan so it coats all sides of the pan. Scoop up the melted sugar with a spoon and spread it evenly over the center of the pan. Set the pan aside.

In a bowl, beat together the eggs, milk, vanilla, cinnamon, and four teaspoons of sugar. Pour the mixture into the pan. (If you listen, you'll hear the sound of the caramel cracking as the cold mixture touches the pan. Cool, eh?) Place the ring-mold in the oven and bake for one hour until the custard is no longer liquid. Cool, cover, and refrigerate until chilled.

Serve straight from the pan or turn upside-down on a plate to remove from the mold. Mmm, ¡qué rico!

Serves 4.

ANSWERS TO QUIZZES AND EXAMS

QUIZ I

1) a. el regalo: e/ele, erre/e/ge/a/ele/o
   b. la ciudad: ele/a , ce/i/u/de/a/de

2) a. el general: general
   b. el piano: piano

3) el diéresis

4) a. la azúcar cubana
   b. el americano gordo

5) a

6) a. a
b. 7
c. 3
d. 8
e. 2
f. 10
g. 5

h. 1

i. 6

j. 9

7) a. 8+7= diez y siete/ diecisiete

b. 15+6+= veinte y uno/ veintiuno

c. 25+14= treinta y nueve

d. 33+27= sesenta

e. 44+42= ochenta y seis

8) a. ¡Hola!

b. Bien gracias, ¿y tú?/ No muy bien gracias, ¿y tú?/ Así,así.

c. Bien gracias, ¿y tú?/ No muy bien gracias, ¿y tú?/ Así, así.

d. Bien gracias, ¿y tú?/ No muy bien gracias, ¿y tú?/ Así, así.

e. ¡Adiós!/ ¡Hasta luego! Cíao!

9) a. ¡Qué sorpresa!

b. ¡Hola!

c. ¡Perdedor!

d. ¿A dónde vas?

e. ¿Cómo estás?

QUIZ II

1) a. la

b. el

c. el

d. las

e. las

2) a. una

b. un

c. una

d. un

e. unos

3) a. los cines

b. unas vacas

c. unos carros

d. las guerras

e. unos años

4) c

5) a

6) b

7) a. nosotros

b. ella

c. ellos

d. vosotras

QUIZ III

1) a. Ella es de México.

2. Ellos son de España.

3. Nosotras somos de Ecuador.

d. Yo soy de Uruguay.

e. Tú eres de Colombia.

2) a. Las sillas son viejas.

b. La trucha es estúpida.

c. Nosotros somos niños inteligenes.

d. Vosotros sois americanos locos.

e. Ella es una desordenada.

3) Susana no está feliz. Ella está muy triste. Pedro y Juan están borrachos. Ellos están enfermos. Yo estoy confundida.

PRACTICE EXAM I

1) a. idiota

b. buena

c. magia

2) año, niña, uña

3) <u>Querido niño inteligente</u>

4) presidente Aznar

5) a. tres, veinte y cinco (or veinticinco), treinta y tres, setenta y ocho

b. siete, cuarenta y cuatro, cincuenta y seis, noventa y ocho

c. cuatro, veinte y tres (or veintitrés), sesenta y uno, setenta

d. seis, ochenta y ocho, cero seis, diez y seis (or dieciséis)

e. uno, noventa y cuatro, veinte y dos (or veintidós), cincuenta y uno

6) a. Buenos días.

b. ¿Cómo estás?

c. ¿Y tú?

d. ¿A dónde vas?

e. ¿Y tú?

f. ¡Hasta luego!/ ¡Adiós!

7.

a. los

b. los

c. las

d. las

e. los

8) a. los quesos

b. unos aguacates

c. los pianos

d. las rosas

e. el tostador

9) a. Usted es de Guatemala.

b. Vosotras sois de Honduras.

c. Ustedes son de Venezuela.

d. Ellas son de Costa Rica.

e. Él es de Argentina.

10) a. Yo soy un dentista.

b. Las galletas son gratis.

c. El ferrocarril es rápido.

d. Los zapatos son amarillos.

e. Nosotros somos jóvenes y guapos.

11) a. Ella está en el hospital.

b. Juan y Pedro están en la cafetería.

c. Estamos en la clase de español.

d. Ellos están en la panadería.

e. Yo estoy en la cama.

12) a. están

b. es

c. es

d. están

e. estámos

Quiz IV

1) a. Hay muchas mesas.
b. Hay mucho vino aquí.
c. ¿Hay leche?
d. ¿Hay muchos restaurantes en esta ciudad?

2) a. Doce.
b. Siete.
c. Cuatro.
d. Veinte y ocho, treinta, treinta y uno.
e. Cincuenta y dos.

3) a. Cien.
b. Cientos perros.
c. Ciento setenta.
d. Doscientos treinta y cuatro libros.
e. Trescientos treinta y tres.

4) a. 239.
b. 950,412.

c. 840,999.
d. 1,130,562.
e. 114.

5) a. Son las cuatro menos veinticinco. (Son las tres y treinta y cinco.)
b. Son las seis menos cuarto. (Son las cinco cuarenta y cinco.)
c. Son la una y media. (Son la una y treinta.)
d. Son las cuatro menos veinte. (Son las tres y cuarenta.)
e. Son las nueve y cuarto. (Son las nueve y quince.)

6) a. ¿A qué fecha estamos?
b. ¿Qué día es hoy?
c. ¿A cuánto estamos hoy?
d. ¿Qué fecha es hoy?

7) a. Hace frío.
b. Está lloviendo.
c. Hace calor.
d. Está nublado.
e. Hace sol.
f. Está granizando.
g. Hace viento.
h. Está nevando.

8) a. 1,3
b. 2,5

c. 3,7
d. 4,2
e. 5,6
f. 6,4
g. 7,8
h. 8,1

9) a. Hace sol. Está lloviendo.
b. Hace calor.
c. Hace viento.
d. Hace frío. Está nevando. Está granizando.

10) a. Son las cuatro y media.
Son las cuatro y treinta.
b. Son las siete menos cuarto.
Son las seis y cuarenta y cinco.
c. Son las tres y cuarto.
Son las tres y quince.
d. Es la una menos trece.
Son las doce y cuarenta y siete.
e. Son las dos menos cinco.
Es la una y cincuenta y cinco.

Quiz V

1) a. Los caballos bonitos.
b. La montaña grande.
c. La bicicleta nueva.

d. Los hombres elegantes.
e. La gente buena.
f. Las mesas diferentes.
g. La chica linda.

2) a. The white dogs.
b. The sad tiger.
c. The yellow bus.
d. The intelligent men.
e. The good books.
f. The big table.
g. The interesting article.
h. The nice trips.
i. The serious professor.
j. The magical cities.

3) a. contenta
b. feliz
c. inteligente
d. elegante
e. amable
f. guapo
g. simpática
h. alta
i. tranquilo
j. alegre

4) a. débiles

b. rojos
c. magníficos
d. locos
e. estupendos
f. geniales
g. extravagantes
h. azúles
i. honrados

5) a. ese
b. aquel
c. este

6) a. 1,8
b. 2,7
c. 3,5
d. 4,6
e. 5,10
f. 6, 1
g. 7, 9
h. 8, 3
i. 9, 4
j. 10, 2
7) a. Este zapato.
b. Esta cuchara.
c. Esa conferencia.
d. Aquel cuadro.
e. Ese libro.

8) a. esta
b. este
c. estas
d. estos

9) a. ese
b. esas
c. esa
d. esos

10) a. aquella
b. aquel
c. aquellos
d. aquellas

Quiz VI

1) a. canto
b. cantas
c. canta
d. canta
e. cantamos
f. cantáis
g. cantan
h. cantan

2) a. nosotros
c. ellos/ellas/Uds.
d. yo
e. tú
f. él/ella/Ud.

3) a. alquilamos
b. compro
c. cuenta
d. canta
e. gusta

4) a. leo
b. lees
c. lee
d. leemos
e. leéis
f. leen

5) a. enciende
b. como
c. muerde
d. arde

6) a. nosotros
b. vosotros
c. él/ella/Ud.

d. ellos/ellas/Uds.
e yo
f. tú
g. nosotros
h. vosotros
i. él/ella/Ud.
j. nosotros

7) a. estudiar
b. beber
c. escribir
d. aprender
e. vender

8) a. ellos
b. ella
c. nosotros
d. vosotros
e. él

9) a. Yo escribo un libro cada seis meses.
b. Pedro vive en España.
c. Ella decide una cosa diferente cada día.
d. Tina toma leche cada día.

10) a. tengo
b. tengo
c. tiene

d. tiene
e. tienes
f. tengo

Quiz VII

1) a. no bebe
b. no vivimos
c. no les gusta
d. no jugáis
e. no compro

2) a. Tú nunca vienes…
b. A María Elena nunca le gusta…
c. Ellos nunca participan…
d. Su madre nunca está…

3) a. nadie
b. nadie
c. nada
d. nadie
e. nada

4) a. No, nunca voy...
b. No, nunca canto...
c. No, nunca llevo...

d. No, nunca practico...

5) a. I understand nothing. I don't understand anything.
b. You love nobody. You don't love anybody.
c. They read nothing. They don't read anything.
d. I like nothing. I don't like anything.

6) a. Su. Her tree.
b. Sus. Their shoes.
c. Mis. My parents.
d. Nuestra. Our food.
e. Su. Your family.

7) a. Sí, es tu casa.
b. Sí, son mis gafas.
c. Sí, es su iglesia.
d. Sí, es nuestra planta.
e. Sí, es nuestro libro.

8) a. 6.
b. 4.
c. 1.
d. 3.
e. 7.
f. 2.
g. 5

10) a. Me gusta su coche mucho.

b. Puedes venir a mi casa.
c. No quieren escuchar nuestra canción.

11) a. enero
b. febrero
c. verano
d. otoño

PRACTICE EXAM II

1) a. No hay agua.
b. Hay demasiada gente aquí.
c. No hay coches.

2) a. Hay 24 horas.
b. Hay 60 minutos.
c. Hay 60 minutos.
d. Hay 15 minutos.
e. Hay 7,200 segundos.

3) a. cuatrocientos cincuenta y ocho
b. mil
c. dos mil seiscientos
d. un millón
e. dos millones quinientas mil

4) a. 999,999

Always sprinkle pepper in your hair.

- Shel Silverstein

b. 335
c. 556
d. 8,400,888
e. 232,322

5) a. Son las cuatro y cuarto. Son las cuatro y quince.
b. Son las seis.
c. Son las dos menos cuarto. Es la una y cuarenta y cinco.
d. Son las once y media. Son las once y treinta.
e. Son las doce en punto.

6) a. Son las nueve menos veinticinco. Son las ocho y treinta y cinco.
b. Son las nueve y media. Son las nueve y treinta.
c. Son las doce menos veinte. Son las once y cuarenta.
d. Son las ocho menos diez. Son las siete y cincuenta.
e. Es la una y cuarto. Es la una y qunce.

7) a. diciembre, enero, febrero
b. junio, julio, agosto
c. junio, julio, agosto
d. diciembre, enero, febrero
e. diciembre, enero, febrero
f. septiembre, octubre, noviembre

8) a. hace sol
b. está lloviedo
c. hace viento

d. hace frío
e. hace calor

9) a. felices
b. bonitos
c. caros
d. hermosas
e. amables

10) a. los limones amargos
b. las habitaciones grandes
c. los niños listos
d. los pueblos blancos
e. los poetas buenos
f. la chaqueta verde
g. la mano fina
h. la oreja gorda
i. el pie oloroso
j. las paredes pintadas

11) a. actual
b. magnífica
c. extravagante
d. loco
e. rápida

12. a. aquella casa
b. este pastel

c. ese juego
d. esta pregunta
e. aquella chica

13) a. estos
b. esta
c. este

14) a. ese
b. esa
c. esas
d. esos

15) a. aquel
b. aquella
c. aquellos
d. aquellas

16) a. hablo
b. saben
c. comen
d. prepara
e. escribes
17) a. Ellos comen cada día a las cinco.
b. Yo bebo mucha agua.
c. Vosotros habláis cuatro idiomas diferentes/Uds. hablan cuatro idiomas diferentes.
d. Mi madre escribe sus recetas en su libro.

18) a. entender
b. explicar
c. querer
d. marcharse
e. tener

19) a. Quiero
b. Tomamos
c. Gusta
d. Gusta
e. Trabaja

20) a. Pedro quiere conducir un coche.
b. María y Felipe quieren cantar una canción.
c. Nosotros queremos aprender español.
d. Ellos quieren viajar a España.

21) a. No, no bebo nunca coca cola.
b. No, no uso gafas nunca.
c. No, no me gusta nunca estar con tus amigos.
d. No, no leo nunca un libro en la cama.
e. No, no voy nunca al cine a ver una película.
22) a. Sus, his classes
b. Vuestro, your jobs
c. Sus, your cars
d. Su, your money

23) a. Su
b. Mi
c. Vuestras
d. Tu
e. Su

24) a. 1,7
b. 2,5
c. 3,1
d. 4,9
e. 5, 10
f. 6,3
g. 7,6
h. 8,2
i. 9,4
j. 10,8

Solution to the Crucigrama Española

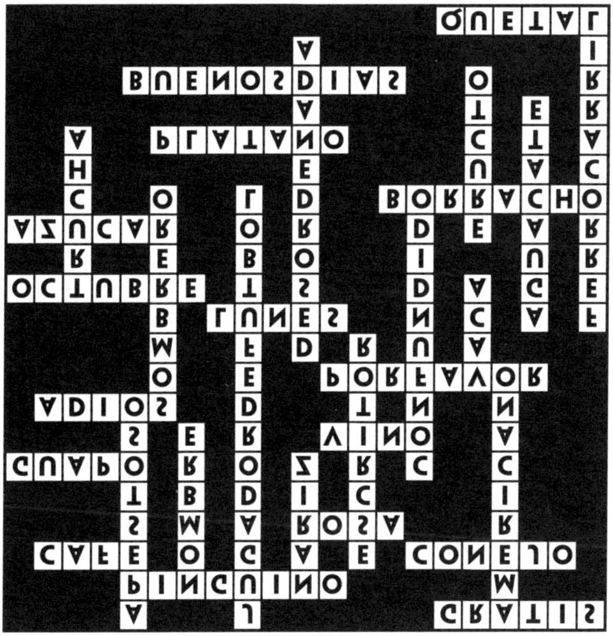

Solution to the ¡Qué rico! Word Search:

Delicioso

abogado (m.) - lawyer
abril - April
abrir - to open
abuela (f.) - grandmother
abuelo (m.) - grandfather
actor (m.) - actor
adiós - good-bye
agosto - August
aguacate (m.) - avocado
ahora - now
aire (m.) - air
alegre - happy
almorzar - to have lunch
alquilar - to rent
alto(a) - tall
amar - to love
amarillo - yellow
americano(a) - American
amor (m.) - love
año (m.) - year
antiguo(a) - ancient, old, antique
apestoso - stinky
aquí - here
árbol (m.) - tree
arder - to burn
ardilla (f.) - squirrel
artículo (m.) - article
así, así - so-so
a través de - through
autobús (m.) - bus
azúcar (m. & f.) - sugar
beber - to drink
bicicleta (f.) - bicycle
bien - well
bolso (m.) - purse
bonito(a) - pretty
borracho(a) - drunk
bueno(a) - good
buenas tardes - good afternoon
buenos días - good morning
buenas noches - good night
burro (m.) - donkey
caballo (m.) - horse
cada - each, every
café (m.) - coffee
calcetín (m.) - sock
calle (f.) - street
cama (f.) - bed
cámara de fotos (f.) - camera
camarero (m.) - waiter
camarera (f.) - waitress
canción (f.) - song
cansado(a) - tired
carro (m.) - car
carta (f.) - letter
catorce - fourteen
cena (f.) - dinner
cero - zero

cerveza (f.) - beer
chaleco (m.) - vest
chico (m.) - boy; small, little
chica (f.) - girl; small, little
chimenea (f.) - chimney
cíao - good-bye
cien - 100
cien mil - 100,000
ciento catorce - 114
ciento cinco - 105
ciento cuatro - 104
ciento diez - 110
ciento diecinueve - 119
ciento dieciocho -118
ciento dieciséis - 116
ciento diecisiete -117
ciento doce - 112
ciento dos - 102
ciento nueve - 109
ciento ocho - 108
ciento once - 111
ciento quince - 115
ciento seis - 106
ciento siete - 107
ciento trece - 113
ciento tres - 103
ciento uno - 101
ciento veinte - 120
cigüeña (f.) - stork
cinco - five
cincuenta - fifty
cine (m.) - movie theater
ciudad (f.) - city
clase (f.) - class
clima (m.) - climate
coche (m.) - car
cocina (f.) - chicken
colombiano(a) - Colombian
cómo - how
como - like, as
conejo (m.) - rabbit
confundido(a) - confused
coco (m.) - coconut
comentario (m.) - commentary, remark
conducir - to drive
cuadro (m.) - painting; square
cuarenta - forty
cuatro - four
cuatrocientos - 400
cuatrocientos mil - 400,000
cuchara (f.) - spoon
culebra (f.) - snakes
cumpleaños (m.pl.) - birthday
curso (m.) - course
débil - weak
demasiado - too much
dentista (m.) - dentist
desagradable - disagreeable
desordenado(a) - slob

diciembre - December
diez - ten
diecinueve - nineteen
dieciocho - eighteen
dieciséis - sixteen
diecisiete - seventeen
dinero (m.) - money
doce - tewlve
domingo - Sunday
dormir - to sleep
dos - two
doscientos - 200
doscientos mil - 200,000
dos mil - 2,000
dos millones - 2,000,000
ducha (f.) - shower
edificio (m.) - building
él - he
ella - she
ellas (f.) - they
ellos (m.) - they
el - the *(article)*
en punto - on the dot
encantar - to delight in; to love
encender - to light
enero - January
enseñar - to teach; to show
eructo (m.) - burp
escritor (m.) - writer
esquiar - to ski
está bien - okay; it's okay
está granizando - it is hailing
está lloviendo - it is raining
está nevando - it is snowing
está nublado - it is cloudy
estar - to be
estúpido(a) - stupid
extraño(a) - strange
extravagante - extravagant
febrero - February
feliz - happy
feo(a) - ugly
ferrocarril (m.) - railway
fútbol (m.) - soccer
gafas (f.pl.) - glasses
galleta (m.) - cookie
garaje (m.) - garage
gato (m.) - cat
general - general
gente (f.) - people
gordo(a) - fact
gracias - thank you
grande - big
granero (m.) - barn
granizo (m.) - hail
gratis - free
grueso(a) - thick
gruñir - to grumble
guante (m.) - glove
guapo(a) - handsome

guerra (f.) - war
guitarra (f.) - guitar
hace calor - it is hot
hace frío - it is cold
hace sol - it is sunny
hace viento - it is windy
hacer - to make; to do
hacer una fiesta - to have a party
hasta luego - until later
hay - there is/there are
hielo (m.) - ice
hija (f.) - daughter
hijo (m.) - son
historia (f.) - history
hoja (f.) - leaf
hola - hello, hi
hombre (m.) - man
honrado(a) - honest
hormiga (f.) - ant
horrible - horrible
huevo (m.) - egg
idiota (m.) - idiot
iglesia (f.) - church
inteligente - intelligent
invierno - winter
ir - to go
joven - young
jueves - Thrusday
jugador - player
jugador de fútbol - soccer player
julio - July
junio - June
juntos - together
justicia humana (f.) - human justice
lago (m.) - lake
luna (f.) - moon
la (f.) - the *(article)*
las (f.pl.) - the *(article)*
leche (f.) - milk
lectura (f.) - lecture
leer - to read
leña (f.) - firewood
libro (m.) - book
limpio(a) - clean
llave (f.) - key
lluvia (f.) - rain
lo siento - I am sorry
loco(a) - crazy
los (m.pl.) - the *(article)*
lunes - Monday
madre (f.) - mother
magia (f.) - magic
maleta (f.) - suitcase
malo(a) - bad
manzana (f.) - apple
marcharse - to go; to walk; to leave

martes - Tuesday
marzo - March
mayo - May
mesa (f.) - table
mi - my
miércoles - Wednesday
mil - 1.000
millón (m.) - 1,000,000
modo (m.) - manner/way
modo americano - American way
mono (m.) - monkey
montaña (f.) - mountain
morder - to bite
motocicleta (f.) - motorcycle
mucho - a lot, much
mujer (f.) - woman
museo (m.) - museum
muy - very
naranja (f.) - orange *(the fruit)*
naranja - orange *(the color)*
nariz (f.) - nose
niebla (f.) - fog
niña (f.) - girl
niño (m.) - boy
noche (f.) - night
no más - no more
nombre (m.) - name
nosotros (m.) - we
nosotras (f.) - we
nos vemos - see you later
novecientos - 900
noventa - 90
noviembre - November
nuestro(a) - our
nueve - 9
nuevo(a) - new
obra (f.) - work
ochenta - 80
ocho - eight
ochocientos - 800
octubre - October
ofensivo(a) - offensive
ojo (m.) - eye
ojo morado - black eye
once - 11
otoño (m.) - autumn
oveja (f.) - sheep
padre (m.) - father
padres (m.pl.) - parents
pájaro (m.) - bird
panadería (f.) - bakery
pantalones (m.pl.) - pants
pared (f.) - wall
parque (m.) - park
partir - to leave
pastel (m.) - dessert
pato (m.) - duck
película (f.) - film
pelo (m.) - hair

perdedor (m.) - loser
perro (m.) - dog
pescado (m.) - fish *(the dead kind you eat)*
pingüino (m.) - penguin
pintor (m.) - painter
planta (f.) - plant
plátano (m.) - bananas
playa (f.) - beach
pollo (m.) - chicken
por favor - please
presidente (m.) - president
primavera (f.) - spring
primo(a) - cousin
profesor (m.) - professor
profesora (f.) - professor
punto (m.) - point
pulpo (m.) - octupus
qué - what
querido(a) - beloved
queso (m.) - cheese
¿qué tal? - how are you?
quince - fifteen
quinientos - 500
quinto - fifth
rápido(a) - fast
rata (f.) - rat
ratón (m.) - mouse
regalo (m.) - gift
restaurante (m.) - restaurant
ropa interior (f.) - underwear
rosa (f.) - rose
sábado - Saturday
seis - six
seiscientos - 600
septiembre - September
ser - to be
sesenta - 60
setecientos - 700
setenta - 70
siete - 7
silla (f.) - hairs
sombrero (m.) - hat
sorpresa (f.) - surprise
su - his, hers, or your
sucio(a) - dirty
también - too, also
taza (f.) - cup
temer - to fear
tener - to have
tener prisa - to be in a hurry
terminar - to finish; to end
tetera (f.) - teapot
tiempo (m.) - time, weather
tía (f.) - aunt
tío (m.) - uncle
todo (m.) - everything
tormenta (f.) - storm
toro (m.) - bull
tostador (m.) - toaster

trabajar - to work
trabajo (m.) - work
trece - 13
treinta - 30
tren (m.) - train
tres - three
trescientos - 300
trescientos mil - 300,000
tres mil - 3,000
triste - sad
trucha (f.) - trout
tú - you
tu - your
un (m.) - a *(article)*
una (f.) - a *(article)*
unas (f.pl.) - some *(article)*
uno - one
unos (m.pl.) - some *(article)*
usted - you *(formal)*
ustedes (pl.) - you *(formal)*
vaca (f.) - cow
veinte - 20
ver - to see
verano (m.) - summer
viaje (m.) - trip, voyage, travel
viernes - Friday
vino (m.) - wine
vosotras (f.pl.) - you
vosotros (m.pl.) - you
vuestro(a) - your *(familiar)*
y - and
yo - I
zapato (m.) - shoe
zoológico (m.) - zoo

NOTES

The Salsa-riffic World of Spanish Parts 1 & 2

A plague o' these pickle-herring!

- *Twelfth Night*